C. S. LEWIS

Readings for
Meditation and Reflection

C. S. LEWIS

Readings
for Meditation
and Reflection

Edited by Walter Hooper

HarperSanFrancisco
An Imprint of HarperCollins*Publishers*

Acknowledgments appear on page 155.

HarperCollins Web Site: http://www.harpercollins.com

HarperCollins®, ☷® and HarperSan Francisco™ are trademarks of HarperCollins Publishers Inc.

FIRST U.S. EDITION

Library of Congress Cataloging-in-Publication Data

Lewis, C. S. (Clive Staples), 1898–1963.
  [Daily readings with C. S. Lewis]
  Readings for meditation and reflection / C. S. Lewis ; edited by Walter Hooper. — 1st U.S. ed.
      p.   cm.
  Originally published: Daily readings with C. S. Lewis. London : Fount, 1992.
  Includes bibliographical references.
  ISBN 0–06–065285–3 (pbk.)
    1. Christian life—Meditations. I. Hooper, Walter. II. Title.
BV4501.2.L468 1996   95–21947
242–dc20   CIP

96 97 98 99 00 ❖ RRD(H) 10 9 8 7 6 5 4 3 2 1

CONTENTS

INTRODUCTION

CLIVE STAPLES LEWIS was born of Church of Ireland parents in an inner suburb of Belfast on 29th November 1898. His father, Albert James Lewis, was a police court solicitor. His mother, Florence Hamilton, was the daughter of the Rector of St Mark's, Dundela, and a graduate of Queen's College in mathematics and logic. The Lewises had one other child, Warren, who was born in 1895. The combination of good Christian parents and a loving elder brother ensured Clive a very happy early childhood. In 1905 the family moved into a larger house, "Little Lea," a few miles away.

Both parents were fond of reading, and it is perhaps not surprising that Clive should give early evidence of his own remarkable ability with words. Before he was two years old his mother said he was "talking like anything." It was not long after this that Clive, disliking the name his parents gave him, announced that he was "Jack"—which name everyone used after that. It was at Little Lea that Jack and Warren created their own imaginary world of "Boxen," and peopled it with characters, both foreshadowing their later careers in literature, Jack as a writer of wide and varied talents and "Warnie" as a historian. It was also as a young boy that the future C. S. Lewis, champion of Reason, emerged. Warnie Lewis has given us an example of that "dexterity of riposte" for which his brother later became so famous. It was 1907 and the family were preparing for a holiday in France. Warnie said, "Entering the study, where my father was poring over his account books, Jack flung himself into a chair and observed, 'I have a prejudice against the French.' My father, interrupted in a long addition sum, said irritably, 'Why?' Jack, crossing his legs and putting his finger tips together, replied, 'If I knew *why* it would not be a prejudice.'"

Two years later the peace of this happy family was destroyed. In 1908 Flora Lewis was found to have cancer, and a few days before she died she gave each of her sons a Bible. Writing about her later in his autobiography, *Surprised by Joy* (1955), C. S. Lewis said that "With my mother's death all settled happiness, all that was tranquil and reliable, disappeared from my life.... It was sea and islands now; the great continent had sunk like Atlantis." For Albert Lewis there seemed no end to the tragedy. His father had died only a few months before his wife, and a favorite brother died a week later.

Jack followed Warnie across the Water to a school called "Wynyard" in Watford, Hertfordshire. It was a terrible introduction to England because the headmaster was insane and very cruel. Jack managed to survive until 1910, when the headmaster had a High Court action brought against him, and the school collapsed. It was at Cherbourg School, overlooking Malvern College, during 1911–1913 that Jack's education began in earnest. But it was also here that he lost his faith. He came under the influence of the School Matron who was, he said, "floundering in the mazes of Theosophy, Rosicrucianism, Spiritualism, the whole Anglo-American Occultist tradition." "Little by little," he wrote, "she loosened the whole framework, blunted all the sharp edges, of my belief.... The whole thing became a matter of speculation: I was soon altering 'I believe' to 'one does feel.'" By the time Lewis entered Malvern College in 1913 he was an apostate.

Jack's loss of faith was to remain hidden from his father. However, during the time he spent at Malvern, and later with a tutor, W. T. Kirkpatrick, in Surrey, his atheism began to take shape. Writing to his friend, Arthur Greeves, in 1916 Jack announced: "I believe in no religion. There is absolutely no proof for any of them, and from a philosophical standpoint Christianity is not even the best. All religions, that is, all mythologies to give them their proper name, are merely man's own invention."

Lewis came up to University College, Oxford, in 1917 to read Classics. A few months later, however, he joined the Officers' Training Corps and was sent to France as a First Lieutenant in the Somerset Light Infantry. He took part in the Battle of Arras and was wounded on Mount Bernenchon in 1918. During his convalescence he compiled a volume of poems, *Spirits in Bondage* (1919), in which he described God as "a phantom called the Good."

Lewis returned to Oxford in 1919. He brought with him the mother of an army friend he had promised to look after if the friend was killed. Mrs. Moore remained with him for the rest of her life. Lewis performed brilliantly in all his work. He took First Class degrees in three subjects—Honour Moderations, Greats and English. In 1925 he was elected to a Fellowship of English at Magdalen College. He read G. K. Chesterton's *Everlasting Man* and "saw the whole Christian outline of history set out in a form that seemed to me to make sense." At the same time his friends Owen Barfield and J. R. R. Tolkien were helping him to find the answers to the questions which had bothered him for so long, "Where has religion reached its true maturity? Where, if anywhere, have the hints of all Paganism been fulfilled?" An account of his conversion is found in *Surprised by Joy* where he says, "In the Trinity Term of 1929 I gave in, and admitted that God was God, and knelt and prayed: perhaps, that night, the most dejected and reluctant convert in all England."

The theological books of C. S. Lewis are so well known that many have no idea that Lewis earned his living at something entirely different. Besides being a very busy college tutor, in 1936 he published his magisterial *The Allegory of Love: A Study in Medieval Tradition*. This was followed by other outstanding works of literary history and criticism. Lewis was such a popular lecturer in Oxford's English School that his lectures attracted overflow crowds.

Still, it is of course as a Christian that most people know him. He first came to prominence in this way through science fiction. Lewis was quick to realize how this medium could be used to serve God's purpose. In 1938 he published *Out of the Silent Planet*, the first of his three interplanetary novels. The Christian purpose of the book was hidden from all but a few, and from this Lewis discovered that "any amount of theology can be smuggled into people's minds under cover of romance without their knowing it." This was followed by one of Lewis's most famous books—*The Screwtape Letters* (1942). It is a series of delightfully witty letters from Screwtape, who is in the administration of the Infernal Civil Service, to Wormwood, a junior colleague who is engaged in trying to secure the damnation of a young man on Earth. Besides being highly entertaining, *The Screwtape Letters* was a milestone for many whose religion was beset by doubts and hesitations. One critic remarked that Lewis possessed the "rare gift of being able to make righteousness readable."

His first straight work of theology was *The Problem of Pain* (1940). Its combination of orthodoxy and clarity caught the eye of the BBC who, in 1941, commissioned him to write a series of talks on "Right and Wrong: A Clue to the Universe." These broadcasts on Natural Law were so provoking that the BBC urged Lewis to return to the microphone for three further series in 1942–1944. The broadcasts were later published as _Mere Christianity_ (1952), and since that time this immensely readable work of Christian apologetics has sold consistently. Lewis made his purpose clear in the Preface, where he said, "Ever since I became a Christian I have thought that the best, perhaps the only, service I could do for my unbelieving neighbors was to explain and defend the belief that has been common to nearly all Christians at all times. . . . I was not writing to expound something I could call 'my religion,' but to expound 'mere' Christianity, which is what it is and was what it was long before I was born and whether I like it or not." The book abounds in examples of Lewis's ability to put complex matters into language that everyone can understand. A notable one appears in the chapter "The Shocking Alternative" where, tackling the age-old question of whether Jesus was "God or a good man," Lewis said:

xiii

> I am here trying to prevent anyone saying the really foolish thing that people often say about Him: "I'm ready to accept Jesus as a great moral teacher, but I don't accept His claim to be God." That is the one thing we must not say. A man who was merely a man and said the sort of things Jesus said would not be a great moral teacher. He would either be a lunatic—on a level with the man who says he is a poached egg—or else he would be the Devil of Hell. You must make your choice. Either this man was, and is, the Son of God: or else a madman or something worse. You can shut Him up for a fool,

you can spit at Him and kill Him as a demon: or
you can fall at His feet and call Him Lord and God.
But let us not come with any patronizing nonsense
about His being a great human teacher. He has not
left that open to us. He did not intend to.

Mere Christianity communicated the Gospel so effectively that many now saw Lewis as the successor of G. K.
Chesterton. He was often asked to explain his method of
reaching people, and it might be useful to mention some of
the things which gave his apologetics such force. He in-
sisted, first of all: (1) that the only reason for believing
Christianity is because it is true. "Christianity is a state-
ment," he said, "which, if false, is of *no* importance, and, if
true, of infinite importance. The one thing it cannot be is
moderately important." (2) It is supernatural. "Do not attempt," he advised, "to water Christianity down. There
must be no pretense that you can have it with the Supernatural left out. So far as I can see Christianity is precisely
the one religion from which the miraculous cannot be sep-
arated." (3) It should be clear. "Any fool can write *learned*
language," he said. "The vernacular is the real test. If you
can't turn your faith into it, then either you don't understand it or you don't believe it." (4) Modern man has reversed the position between God and himself. "The
ancient man," said Lewis, "approached God (or even the
gods) as the accused person approaches his judge. For the
modern man the roles are reversed. He is the judge: God is
in the dock. He is quite a kindly judge: if God should have
a reasonable defense for being the god who permits war,
poverty and disease, he is ready to listen to it. The trial may
even end in God's acquittal. But the important thing is that
man is on the bench and God in the dock."

It would take a book to cover all that Lewis said and did on behalf of the Faith during the War years. Besides the broadcasts, he had been recruited by the R.A.F. to go to their bases all over the country giving talks on Theology. There were many other invitations to talk and preach, and he felt it part of his "war effort" to accept them all. And always waiting at home for him was an even harder job. This was the daily mail-bag. Over the years he got letters from nearly everywhere. His brother Warnie had lived with him since he retired from the Army in 1930, and with his assistance, Lewis answered every letter by return of post. We'll never know how he managed this. But an account of his actions would not be complete unless it revealed what no one knew until after he died. Beginning with the first money he made from his writings, he had two-thirds of the royalties put into a charity run by his lawyer. Most of it went to widows and orphans who were known to be in need.

Another of Lewis's most successful books came at the end of the War. This was *The Great Divorce: A Dream* (1945), in which the dream consists in Lewis imagining a group of people from Hell visiting Heaven. In contrast to the solidity of Heaven the damned are like dirty smudges on the air. But they learn that if they will surrender to God they will "thicken up" and be able to remain there. Lewis makes himself one of the damned, and when he asks if everyone is given the choice of accepting God or not, he is told: "There are only two kinds of people in the end: those who say to God, 'Thy will be done,' and those to whom God says, in the end, '*Thy* will be done.' All that are in Hell, choose it. Without that self-choice there could be no Hell. No soul that seriously and constantly desires joy will ever miss it. Those who seek find. To those who knock it is opened."

Some think that Lewis's best books were saved till last. They mean, of course, the seven "Chronicles of Narnia." In the first of these fairy stories, *The Lion, the Witch and the Wardrobe* (1950), Lewis introduced his readers to his imaginary world of "Narnia." It is ruled over by a great, royal lion named Aslan, whom some recognize instantly as Christ. Asked how he came to write the Chronicles, Lewis said, "I thought I saw how stories of this kind could steal past a certain inhibition which had paralyzed much of my own religion in childhood. Why did one find it so hard to feel as one was told one ought to feel about God or about the sufferings of Christ? I thought the chief reason was that one was told one ought to. . . . But supposing that by casting all these things into an imaginary world, stripping them of their stained-glass and Sunday School associations, one could make them for the first time appear in their real potency? Could one not thus steal past those watchful dragons? I thought one could."

The Narnian stories are some of the most popular in the world. They are, besides all else, first class stories. However, judging from the many fan letters still written to Lewis, Aslan is the most popular character in the books and the most dearly loved. When one child asked about him, Lewis said, "I'm not exactly 'representing' the real [Christian] story in symbols. I'm more saying, 'Suppose there were a world like Narnia and it needed rescuing and the Son of God (or the Great Emperor-Over-Sea) went to redeem it, as He came to redeem ours, what might it, in that world, all have been like?'"

Although Lewis was very popular with undergraduates and a recognized scholar in his field, he was never given a professional chair in his own university. Many resented his evangelical zeal and the popularity won from such books as *The Screwtape Letters*. However, when his impressive *English Literature in the Sixteenth Century* appeared in 1954, Cambridge University chose him for their new Chair of Medieval and Renaissance English Literature. He accepted the position in 1955, becoming at the same time a Fellow of Magdalene College, Cambridge. Lewis kept his home in Oxford, to which he returned on weekends and during vacations.

Mrs. Moore died in 1951, and the following year Lewis met the American poet Joy Davidman Gresham. Shortly afterwards she divorced her husband and came to live in Oxford with her two sons. In 1956 Lewis married her in the Registry office to prevent her extradition. Soon afterwards Joy appeared to be dying of cancer, and in 1957 they were married by an Anglican clergyman in the hospital. Joy unexpectedly recovered and she and Lewis had several happy years together. It was during this time that Lewis published *The Four Loves* (1960). After Joy died in 1960 Lewis wrote *A Grief Observed* (1960), a short, poignant book about his loss.

By 1963 Lewis had won the respect of the entire Christian family—whether Catholics or Protestants—by his adherence to "the enormous common ground" of essential Christian beliefs, and by his refusal to involve himself in the sectarian squabbles which characterize so much of Christian writing.

Lewis had been ill ever since he lost his wife. Shortly after finishing a book on prayer, *Letters to Malcolm,* he had a heart attack in July 1963 and was in a coma for a day. After he recovered he spent the next few months writing to a few old friends. "I can't help feeling," he said to one, "it was rather a pity I did revive in July. I mean, having been glided so painlessly up to the Gate it seems hard to have it

xvii

INTRODUCTION

shut in one's face and know that the whole process must some day be gone thro' again, and perhaps far less pleasantly! Poor Lazarus! But God knows best." On 22nd November 1963 Lewis died peacefully and quietly at home in Oxford. No one was better prepared.

Walter Hooper

Readings
for Meditation
and Reflection

THE LION AND THE STREAM

"ARE YOU not thirsty?" said the Lion.

"I'm *dying* of thirst," said Jill.

"Then drink," said the Lion.

"May I—could I—would you mind going away while I do?," said Jill.

The Lion answered this only by a look and a very low growl. And as Jill gazed at its motionless bulk, she realized that she might as well have asked the whole mountain to move aside for her convenience.

The delicious rippling noise of the stream was driving her nearly frantic.

"Will you promise not to—do anything to me, if I do come?," said Jill.

"I make no promise," said the Lion.

Jill was so thirsty now that, without noticing it, she had come a step nearer.

"*Do* you eat girls?," she said.

"I have swallowed up girls and boys, women and men, kings and emperors, cities and realms," said the Lion. It didn't say this as if it were boasting, nor as if it were sorry, nor as if it were angry. It just said it.

"I daren't come and drink," said Jill.

"Then you will die of thirst," said the Lion.

"Oh dear!," said Jill, coming another step nearer. "I suppose I must go and look for another stream then."

"There is no other stream," said the Lion.

The Silver Chair
Chapter 2

Readings for Meditation and Reflection

THE INTOLERABLE COMPLIMENT

WHEN we want to be something other than the thing God wants us to be, we must be wanting what, in fact, will not make us happy. Those Divine demands which sound to our natural ears most like those of a despot and least like those of a lover, in fact marshall us where we should want to go if we knew what we wanted. He demands our worship, our obedience, our prostration. Do we suppose that they can do Him any good, or fear like the chorus in Milton, that human irreverence can bring about "His glory's diminution"? A man can no more diminish God's glory by refusing to worship Him than a lunatic can put out the sun by scribbling the word "darkness" on the wall of his cell. . . .

We are bidden to "put on Christ," to become like God. That is, whether we like it or not, God intends to give us what we need, not what we now think we want. Once more, we are embarrassed by the intolerable compliment, by too much love, not too little.

The Problem of Pain
Chapter 3

C. S. LEWIS

THE LORD OF
TERRIBLE ASPECT

WHEN Christianity says that God loves man, it means that God *loves* man: not that He has some "disinterested," because really indifferent, concern for our welfare, but that, in awful and surprising truth, we are the objects of His love. You asked for a loving God: you have one. The great spirit you so lightly invoked, the "lord of terrible aspect," is present: not a senile benevolence that drowsily wishes you to be happy in your own way, not the cold philanthropy of a conscientious magistrate, nor the care of a host who feels responsible for the comfort of his guests, but the consuming fire Himself, the Love that made the worlds, persistent as the artist's love for his work and despotic as a man's love for a dog, jealous, inexorable, exacting as love between the sexes.

The Problem of Pain
Chapter 3

Readings for Meditation and Reflection

THE COST OF DISCIPLESHIP

THE ORDINARY idea which we all have before we become Christians is this. We take as a starting point our ordinary self with its various desires and interests. We then admit that something else—call it "morality" or "decent behaviour" or "the good of society"—has claims on this self; claims which interfere with its own desires. What we mean by "being good" is giving in to those claims. Some of the things the ordinary self wanted to do turn out to be what we call "wrong": well, we must give them up. Other things, which the self did not want to do, turn out to be what we call "right": well, we shall have to do them. But we are hoping all the time that when all the demands have been met, the poor natural self will still have some chance, and some time, to get on with its own life and do what it likes. In fact, we are very like an honest man paying his taxes. He pays them all right, but he does hope that there will be enough left over for him to live on. Because we are still taking our natural self as the starting point.

As long as we are thinking that way, one or other of two results is likely to follow. Either we give up trying to be good, or else we become very unhappy indeed. For, make no mistake: if you are really going to try to meet all the demands made on the natural self, it will not have enough left over to live on. The more you obey your conscience, the more your conscience will demand of you. And your natural self, which is thus being starved and hampered and worried at every turn, will get angrier and angrier. In the end, you will either give up trying to be good, or else become one of those people who, as they say, "live for others" but always in a discontented, grumbling way—

C. S. LEWIS

always wondering why the others do not notice it more, and always making a martyr of yourself. And once you have become that you will be a far greater pest to anyone who has to live with you than you would have been if you had remained frankly selfish.

The Christian way is different: harder, and easier. Christ says, "Give me All. I don't want so much of your time and so much of your money and so much of your work: I want You. I have not come to torment your natural self, but to kill it. No half-measures are any good. I don't want to cut off a branch here and a branch there. I want to have the whole tree down. I don't want to drill the tooth, or crown it, or stop it, but to have it out. Hand over the whole natural self, all the desires which you think innocent as well as the ones you think wicked—the whole outfit. I will give you a new self instead. In fact, I will give you Myself: my own will shall become yours."

Mere Christianity
Book IV Chapter 8

CAN'T YOU LEAD A GOOD LIFE WITHOUT BELIEVING IN CHRISTIANITY?

"CAN'T you lead a good life without believing in Christianity?" This is the question on which I have been asked to write, and straight away, before I begin trying to answer it, I have a comment to make. The question sounds as if it were asked by a person who said to himself, "I don't care whether Christianity is in fact true or not. I'm not interested in finding out whether the real universe is more like what the Christians say than what the Materialists say. All I'm interested in is leading a good life. I'm going to choose beliefs not because I think them true but because I find them helpful."

Now frankly, I find it hard to sympathize with this state of mind. One of the things that distinguishes man from the other animals is that he wants to know things, wants to find out what reality is like, simply for the sake of knowing. When that desire is completely quenched in anyone, I think he has become something less than human. As a matter of fact, I can't believe any of you have really lost that desire. More probably, foolish preachers, by always telling you how much Christianity will help you and how good it is for society, have actually led you to forget that Christianity is not a patent medicine. Christianity claims to give an account of *facts*—to tell you what the real universe is like. Its account of the universe may be true, or it may not, and once the question is really before you, then your natural inquisitiveness must make you want to know the answer. If Christianity is untrue, then no honest man will want to believe it, however helpful it might be: if it is true, every honest man will want to believe it, even if it gives him no help at all.

"Man or Rabbit?"
in *God in the Dock*

Readings for Meditation and Reflection

THE CHRISTIAN
AND THE MATERIALIST

IF CHRISTIANITY should happen to be true, then it is quite impossible that those who know this truth and those who don't should be equally well equipped for leading a good life. Knowledge of the facts must make a difference to one's actions. Suppose you found a man on the point of starvation and wanted to do the right thing. If you had no knowledge of medical science, you would probably give him a large solid meal; and as a result your man would die. In the same way a Christian and a non-Christian may both wish to do good to their fellow men. The one believes that men are going to live for ever, that they were created by God and so built that they can find their true and lasting happiness only by being united to God, that they have gone badly off the rails, and that obedient faith in Christ is the only way back. The other believes that men are an accidental result of the blind working of matter, that they started as mere animals and have more or less steadily improved, that they are going to live for about seventy years, that their happiness is fully attainable by good social services and political organizations, and that everything else (e.g., vivisection, birth-control, the judicial system, education) is to be judged to be "good" or "bad" simply in so far as it helps or hinders that kind of "happiness."

Now there are quite a lot of things which these two men could agree in doing for their fellow citizens. Both would approve of efficient sewers and hospitals and a healthy diet. But sooner or later the difference of their beliefs would produce differences in their practical proposals. Both, for example, might be very keen about education:

C. S. LEWIS

but the kinds of education they wanted people to have would obviously be very different. Again, where the Materialist would simply ask about a proposed action, "Will it increase the happiness of the majority?," the Christian might have to say, "Even if it does increase the happiness of the majority, we can't do it. It is unjust." And all the time, one great difference would run through their whole policy. To the Materialist things like nations, classes, civilizations must be more important than individuals, because the individuals live only seventy odd years each and the group may last for centuries. But to the Christian, individuals are more important, for they live eternally; and races, civilizations and the like, are in comparison the creatures of a day.

The Christian and the Materialist hold different beliefs about the universe. They can't both be right. The one who is wrong will act in a way which simply doesn't fit the real universe. Consequently, with the best will in the world, he will be helping his fellow creatures to their destruction.

"Man or Rabbit?"
in *God in the Dock*

CAN SOMEONE
LEAD A GOOD LIFE
WITHOUT CHRISTIANITY?

THE QUESTION before each of us is not "Can *someone* lead a good life without Christianity?" The question is, "Can *I*?" We all know there have been good men who were not Christians; men like Socrates and Confucius who had never heard of it, or men like J. S. Mill who quite honestly couldn't believe it. . . .

But the man who asks me, "Can't I lead a good life without believing in Christianity?" is clearly not in the same position. If he hadn't heard of Christianity he would not be asking this question. If, having heard of it, and having seriously considered it, he had decided that it was untrue, then once more he would not be asking the question. The man who asks this question has heard of Christianity and is by no means certain that it may not be true. He is really asking, "Need I bother about it? Mayn't I just evade the issue, just let sleeping dogs lie, and get on with being 'good'? Aren't good intentions enough to keep me safe and blameless without knocking at that dreadful door and making sure whether there is, or isn't, someone inside?"

To such a man it might be enough to reply that he is really asking to be allowed to get on with being "good" before he has done his best to discover what *good* means. But that is not the whole story. We need not inquire whether God will punish him for his cowardice and laziness: they will punish themselves. The man is shirking. He is deliberately trying not to know whether Christianity is true or false, because he foresees endless trouble if it should turn

C. S. LEWIS

out to be true. He is like the man who deliberately "forgets" to look at the notice board because, if he did, he might find his name down for some unpleasant duty. . . .

"Man or Rabbit?"
in *God in the Dock*

WILL CHRISTIANITY
HELP ME?

Bᴜᴛ sᴛɪʟʟ—for intellectual honour has sunk very low in our age—I hear someone whimpering on with his question, "Will it help me? Will it make me happy? Do you really think I'd be better if I became a Christian?" Well, if you must have it, my answer is "Yes." But I don't like giving an answer at all at this stage. Here is a door, behind which, according to some people, the secret of the universe is waiting for you. Either that's true, or it isn't. And if it isn't, then what the door really conceals is simply the greatest fraud, the most colossal "sell" on record. Isn't it obviously the job of every man (that is a man and not a rabbit) to try to find out which, and then to devote his full energies either to serving this tremendous secret or to exposing and destroying this gigantic humbug? Faced with such an issue, can you really remain wholly absorbed in your own blessed "moral development"?

All right, Christianity will do you good—a great deal more good than you ever wanted or expected. And the first bit of good it will do you is to hammer into your head (you won't enjoy *that!*) the fact that what you have hitherto called "good"—all that about "leading a decent life" and "being kind"—isn't quite the magnificent and all-important affair you supposed. It will teach you that in fact you can't be "good" (not for twenty-four hours) on your own moral efforts. And then it will teach you that even if you were, you still wouldn't have achieved the purpose for which you were created. Mere *morality* is not the end of life. You were made for something quite different from that. . . . The people who keep on asking if they can't lead a decent life without Christ, don't know what life is about; if they did they would know

C. S. LEWIS

that "a decent life" is mere machinery compared with the thing we men are really made for. Morality is indispensable: but the Divine Life, which gives itself to us and which calls us to be gods, intends for us something in which morality will be swallowed up. We are to be re-made. All the rabbit in us is to disappear—the worried, conscientious, ethical rabbit as well as the cowardly and sensual rabbit. We shall bleed and squeal as the handfuls of fur come out; and then, surprisingly, we shall find underneath it all a thing we have never yet imagined: a real Man, an ageless god, a son of God, strong, radiant, wise, beautiful, and drenched in joy.

"Man or Rabbit?"
in *God in the Dock*

FIRST AND SECOND THINGS

THE WOMAN who makes a dog the centre of her life loses, in the end, not only her human usefulness and dignity but even the proper pleasure of dog-keeping. The man who makes alcohol his chief good loses not only his job but his palate and all power of enjoying the earlier (and only pleasurable) levels of intoxication. It is a glorious thing to feel for a moment or two that the whole meaning of the universe is summed up in one woman— glorious so long as other duties and pleasures keep tearing you away from her. But clear the decks and so arrange your life (it is sometimes feasible) that you will have nothing to do but contemplate her, and what happens? Of course this law has been discovered before, but it will stand re-discovery. It may be stated as follows: every preference of a small good to a great, or a partial good to a total good, involves the loss of the small or partial good for which the sacrifice was made.

Apparently the world is made that way. If Esau really got the pottage in return for his birthright, then Esau was a lucky exception. You can't get second things by putting them first; you can get second things only by putting first things first. From which it would follow that the question, "What things are first?" is of concern not only to philosophers but to everyone.

It is impossible in this context, not to inquire what our own civilization has been putting first for the last thirty years. And the answer is plain. It has been putting itself first. To preserve civilization has been the great aim; the collapse of civilization, the great bugbear. Peace, a high standard of life, hygiene, transport, science and amusement—all these, which are what we usually mean by civilization, have been our ends. It will be replied that our concern for civilization is very natural and very necessary at a time when civilization is so imperilled. But how if the shoe is on the other foot?—how if civilization has been imperilled precisely by the fact that we have all made civilization our *summum bonum*? Perhaps it can't be preserved in that way. Perhaps civilization will never be safe until we care for something else more than we care for it.

The hypothesis has certain facts to support it. As far as peace (which is one ingredient in our idea of civilization) is concerned, I think many would now agree that a foreign policy dominated by desire for peace is one of the many roads that lead to war. And was civilization ever seriously endangered until civilization became the exclusive aim of human activity? There is much rash idealization of past ages about, and I do not wish to encourage more of it. Our ancestors were cruel, lecherous, greedy and stupid, like ourselves. But while they cared for other things more than for civilization—and they cared at different times for all sorts of things, for the will of God, for glory, for personal honour, for doctrinal purity, for justice—was civilization often in serious danger of disappearing?

At least the suggestion is worth a thought. To be sure, if it were true that civilization will never be safe till it is put second, that immediately raises the question, second to what? What is the first thing? The only reply I can offer here is that if we do not know, then the first, and only truly practical, thing is to set about finding out.

"First and Second Things"
in *First and Second Things*

THE FIRST JOB

THE REAL problem of the Christian life comes where people do not usually look for it. It comes the very moment you wake up each morning. All your wishes and hopes for the day rush at you like wild animals. And the first job each morning consists simply in shoving them all back; in listening to that other voice, taking that other point of view, letting that other larger, stronger, quieter life come flowing in. And so on, all day. Standing back from all your natural fussings and frettings; coming in out of the wind.

We can only do it for moments at first. But from those moments the new sort of life will be spreading through our system: because now we are letting Him work at the right part of us. It is the difference between paint, which is merely laid on the surface, and a dye or stain which soaks right through. He never talked vague, idealistic gas. When He said, "Be perfect," He meant it. He meant that we must go in for the full treatment. It is hard; but the sort of compromise we are all hankering after is harder—in fact, it is impossible. It may be hard for an egg to turn into a bird: it would be a jolly sight harder for it to learn to fly while remaining an egg. We are like eggs at present. And you cannot go on indefinitely being just an ordinary, decent egg. We must be hatched or go bad. . . .

This is the whole of Christianity. There is nothing else. It is so easy to get muddled about that. It is easy to think that the Church has a lot of different objects—education, building, missions, holding services. Just as it is easy to think the State has a lot of different objects—military, political, economic, and what not. But in a way things are much simpler than that. The State exists simply to promote

C. S. LEWIS

and to protect the ordinary happiness of human beings in this life. A husband and wife chatting over a fire, a couple of friends having a game of darts in a pub, a man reading a book in his own room or digging in his own garden—that is what the State is there for. . . .

In the same way the Church exists for nothing else but to draw men into Christ, to make them little Christs. If they are not doing that, all the cathedrals, clergy, missions, sermons, even the Bible itself, are simply a waste of time. God became Man for no other purpose. It is even doubtful, you know, whether the whole universe was created for any other purpose.

Mere Christianity
Book IV Chapter 8

THE INVASION

I s it not frightfully unfair that this new life should be confined to people who have heard of Christ and been able to believe in Him? But the truth is God has not told us what His arrangements about the other people are. We do know that no man can be saved except through Christ; we do not know that only those who know Him can be saved through Him. But in the meantime, if you are worried about the people outside, the most unreasonable thing you can do is to remain outside yourself. Christians are Christ's body, the organism through which He works. Every addition to that body enables Him to do more. If you want to help those outside you must add your own little cell to the body of Christ who alone can help them. Cutting off a man's fingers would be an odd way of getting him to do more work.

Another possible objection is this. Why is God landing in this enemy-occupied world in disguise and starting a sort of secret society to undermine the devil? Why is He not landing in force, invading it? Is it that He is not strong enough? Well, Christians think He is going to land in force; we do not know when. But we can guess why He is delaying. He wants to give us the chance of joining His side freely. I do not suppose you and I would have thought much of a Frenchman who waited till the Allies were marching into Germany and then announced he was on our side. God will invade. But I wonder whether people who ask God to interfere openly and directly in our world quite realize what it will be like when He does. When that happens, it is the end of the world. When the author walks on to the stage the play is over. God is going to invade, all right: but what is the good of saying you are on His side

18

C. S. LEWIS

then, when you see the whole natural universe melting away like a dream and something else—something it never entered your head to conceive—comes crashing in; something so beautiful to some of us and so terrible to others that none of us will have any choice left? For this time it will be God without disguise; something so overwhelming that it will strike either irresistible love or irresistible horror into every creature. It will be too late then to choose your side. There is no use saying you choose to lie down when it has become impossible to stand up. That will not be the time for choosing: it will be the time when we discover which side we really have chosen, whether we realized it before or not. Now, today, this moment, is our chance to choose the right side. God is holding back to give us that chance. It will not last forever. We must take it or leave it.

Mere Christianity
Book II Chapter 5

THE PERSONALITY OF JESUS

I F ANYTHING whatever is common to all believers, and even to many unbelievers, it is the sense that in the gospels they have met a personality. There are characters whom we know to be historical but of whom we do not feel that we have any personal knowledge—knowledge by acquaintance: such as Alexander, Attila or William of Orange. There are others who make no claim to historical reality but whom, none the less, we know as we know real people: Falstaff, Uncle Toby, Mr Pickwick. But there are only three characters who, claiming the first sort of reality, also actually have the second. And surely everyone knows who they are: Plato's Socrates, the Jesus of the gospels, and Boswell's Johnson.

Our acquaintance with them shows itself in a dozen ways. When we look into the Apocryphal gospels, we find ourselves constantly saying of this or that *logion,* "No. It's just a fine saying, but not His. That wasn't how He talked"—just as we do with all pseudo-Johnsoniana. We are not in the least perturbed by the contrasts within each character: the union in Socrates of silly and scabrous titters about Greek pederasty with the highest mystical fervour and homeliest good sense; in Johnson, of profound gravity and melancholy with that love of fun and nonsense which Boswell never understood though Fanny Burney did; in Jesus, of peasant shrewdness, intolerable severity and irresistible tenderness.

So strong is the flavour of the personality that, even while He says things which, on any other assumption than that of Divine Incarnation in the fullest sense, would be appallingly arrogant, yet we—and many unbelievers—accept Him at His own valuation when He says, "I am meek and

C. S. LEWIS

lowly of heart." Even those passages in the New Testament which superficially, and in intention, are most concerned with the Divine, and least with the Human Nature, bring us face to face with the personality. I am not sure that they don't do this more than any others. "We beheld His glory, the glory as of the only begotten of the Father, full of graciousness and reality ... which we have looked upon and our hands have handled."

"Fern-seed and Elephants"
in *Fern-seed and Elephants*

WHAT ARE WE TO
MAKE OF JESUS CHRIST?

WHAT are we to make of Jesus Christ? This is a question which has, in a sense, a frantically comic side. For the real question is not what are we to make of Christ, but what is He to make of us? The picture of a fly sitting deciding what it is going to make of an elephant has comic elements about it. But perhaps the questioner meant, what are we to make of Him in the sense of "How are we to solve the historical problem set us by the recorded sayings and acts of this Man?" This problem is to reconcile two things. On the one hand you have got the almost generally admitted depth and sanity of His moral teaching, which is not very seriously questioned, even by those who are opposed to Christianity. In fact, I find when I am arguing with very anti-God people that they rather make a point of saying, "I am entirely in favour of the moral teaching of Christianity"—and there seems to be a general agreement that in the teaching of this Man and of His immediate followers, moral truth is exhibited at its purest and best. It is not sloppy idealism, it is full of wisdom and shrewdness. The whole thing is realistic, fresh to the highest degree, the product of a sane mind. That is one phenomenon.

The other phenomenon is the quite appalling nature of this Man's theological remarks. You all know what I mean, and I want rather to stress the point that the appalling claim which this Man seems to be making is not merely made at one moment of His career. There is, of course, the one moment which led to His execution. The moment at which the High Priest said to Him, "Who are

C. S. LEWIS

you?" "I am the Anointed, the Son of the uncreated God, and you shall see Me appearing at the end of all history as the judge of the Universe." But that claim, in fact, does not rest on this one dramatic moment. When you look into His conversation you will find this sort of claim running through the whole thing. For instance, He went about saying to people, "I forgive your sins." Now it is quite natural for a man to forgive something you do to *him*. Thus if somebody cheats me out of £5 it is quite possible and reasonable for me to say, "Well, I forgive him, we will say no more about it." What on earth would you say if somebody had done *you* out of £5 and *I* said, "That is all right, I forgive him"? Then there is a curious thing which seems to slip out almost by accident. On one occasion this Man is sitting looking down on Jerusalem from the hill above it, and suddenly in comes an extraordinary remark—"I keep on sending you prophets and wise men." Nobody comments on it. And yet, quite suddenly, almost incidentally, He is claiming to be the power that all through the centuries is sending wise men and leaders into the world. Here is another curious remark: in almost every religion there are unpleasant observances like fasting. This Man suddenly remarks one day, "No one need fast while I am here." Who is this Man who remarks that His mere presence suspends all normal rules? Who is the person who can suddenly tell the School they can have a half-holiday? Sometimes the statements put forward the assumption that He, the Speaker, is completely without sin or fault. This is always the attitude. "You, to whom I am talking, are all sinners," and He never remotely suggests that this same reproach can be brought against Him. He says again, "I am begotten of the One God, before Abraham was, I am," and remember what the words "I am" were in Hebrew. They were the name of God, which must not be spoken by any human being, the name which it was death to utter.

"What are we to make of Jesus Christ?"
in *God in the Dock*

C. S. LEWIS

CHRIST HAS NO PARALLEL
IN OTHER RELIGIONS

ON THE one side clear, definite moral teaching. On the other, claims which, if not true, are those of a megalomaniac, compared with whom Hitler was the most sane and humble of men. There is no half-way house and there is no parallel in other religions. If you had gone to Buddha and asked him, "Are you the son of Bramah?," he would have said, "My son, you are still in the vale of illusion." If you had gone to Socrates and asked, "Are you Zeus?," he would have laughed at you. If you had gone to Mohammed and asked, "Are you Allah?" he would first have rent his clothes and then cut your head off. If you had asked Confucius, "Are you Heaven?," I think he would have probably replied, "Remarks which are not in accordance with nature are in bad taste." The idea of a great moral teacher saying what Christ said is out of the question. In my opinion, the only person who can say that sort of thing is either God or a complete lunatic suffering from that form of delusion which undermines the whole mind of man. If you think you are a poached egg, when you are looking for a piece of toast to suit you, you may be sane, but if you think you are God, there is no chance for you. We may note in passing that He was never regarded as a mere moral teacher. He did not produce that effect on any of the people who actually met Him. He produced mainly three effects—Hatred—Terror—Adoration. There was no trace of people expressing mild approval.

What are we to do about reconciling the two contradictory phenomena? One attempt consists in saying that

the man did not really say these things, but that His followers exaggerated the story, and so the legend grew up that
he had said them. This is difficult because His followers
were all Jews; that is, they belonged to that nation which of
all others was most convinced that there was only one
God—that there could not possibly be another. It is very
odd that this horrible invention about a religious leader
should grow up among the one people in the whole earth
least likely to make such a mistake. On the contrary, we get
the impression that none of His immediate followers or
even of the New Testament writers embraced the doctrine
at all easily.

Another point is that on that view you would have
to regard the accounts of the Man as being *legends*. Now,
as a literary historian, I am perfectly convinced that whatever else the gospels are they are not legends. I have read a
great deal of legend and I am quite clear that they are not
the same sort of thing. They are not artistic enough to be
legends. From an imaginative point of view they are
clumsy, they don't work up to things properly. Most of the
life of Jesus is totally unknown to us, as is the life of anyone else who lived at that time, and no people building up
a legend would allow that to be so. Apart from bits of the
Platonic dialogues, there are no conversations that I know
of in ancient literature like the Fourth Gospel. There is
nothing, even in modern literature, until about a hundred
years ago when the realistic novel came into existence. In
the story of the woman taken in adultery we are told
Christ bent down and scribbled in the dust with His finger. Nothing comes of this. No one has ever based any
doctrine on it. And the act of *inventing* little irrelevant de-
tails to make an imaginary scene more convincing is a

purely modern art. Surely the only explanation of this passage is that the thing really happened? The author put it in simply because he had seen it.

"What are we to make of Jesus Christ?"
in *God in the Dock*

27

GOD HAS COME DOWN INTO
THE CREATED UNIVERSE

WE COME to the strangest story of all, the story of the Resurrection. It is very necessary to get the story clear. I heard a man say, "The importance of the Resurrection is that it gives evidence of survival, evidence that the human personality survives death." On that view, what happened to Christ would be what had always happened to all men, the difference being that in Christ's case we were privileged to see it happening. This is certainly not what the earliest Christian writers thought. Something perfectly new in the history of the Universe had happened. Christ had defeated death. The door which had always been locked had for the very first time been forced open. This is something quite distinct from mere ghost-survival. I don't mean that they disbelieved in ghost-survival. On the contrary, they believed in it so firmly that, on more than one occasion, Christ had had to assure them that He was *not* a ghost. The point is that while believing in survival they yet regarded the Resurrection as something totally different and new. The Resurrection narratives are not a picture of survival after death; they record how a totally new mode of being has arisen in the Universe. Something new had appeared in the Universe: as new as the first coming of organic life. This Man, after death, does not get divided into "ghost" and "corpse." A new mode of being has arisen. That is the story. What are we going to make of it?

The question is, I suppose, whether any hypothesis covers the facts so well as the Christian hypothesis. That hypothesis is that God has come down into the created universe, down to manhood—and come up again, pulling it up with Him. The alternative hypothesis is not legend, nor exaggeration, nor the apparitions of a ghost. It is either lunacy or lies. Unless one can take the second alternative (and I can't) one turns to the Christian theory.

"What are we to make of Christ?" There is no question of what we can make of Him, it is entirely a question of what He intends to make of us. You must accept or reject the story.

The things He says are very different from what any other teacher has said. Others say, "This is the truth about the Universe. This is the way you ought to go," but He says, "I am the Truth, and the Way, and the Life." He says, "No man can reach absolute reality, except through Me. Try to retain your own life and you will be inevitably ruined. Give yourself away and you will be saved." He says, "If you are ashamed of Me, if, when you hear this call, you turn the other way, I also will look the other way when I come again as God without disguise. If anything whatever is keeping you from God and from Me, whatever it is, throw it away. If it is your eye, pull it out. If it is your hand, cut if off. If you put yourself first you will be last. Come to Me everyone who is carrying a heavy load, I will set that right. Your sins, all of them, are wiped out, I can do that. I am Re-birth. I am Life. Eat me, drink Me, I am your Food. And finally, do not be afraid, I have overcome the whole Universe." That is the issue.

"What are we to make of Jesus Christ?"
in *God in the Dock*

SCREWTAPE EXPLAINS HELL'S INVENTION OF THE "HISTORICAL JESUS"

You will find that a good many Christian-political writers think that Christianity began going wrong, and departing from the doctrine of its Founder, at a very early stage. Now this idea must be used by us to encourage once again the conception of a "historical Jesus" to be found by clearing away later "accretions and perversions" . . . The advantages of these constructions, which we intend to change every thirty years or so, are manifold.

In the first place, they all tend to direct men's devotion to something which does not exist, for each "historical Jesus" is unhistorical. The documents say what they say and cannot be added to; each new "historical Jesus" therefore has to be got out of them by suppression at one point and exaggeration at another. In the second place, all such constructions place the importance of their Historical Jesus in some peculiar theory He is supposed to have promulgated. He has to be a "great man" in the modern sense of the word—one standing at the terminus of some centrifugal and unbalanced line of thought—a crank vending a panacea. We thus distract men's minds from Who He is, and what He did. We first make Him solely a teacher, and then conceal the very substantial agreement between His teachings and those of all other great moral teachers. For humans must not be allowed to notice that all great moralists are sent by the Enemy not to inform men but to remind them, to restate the primeval moral platitudes against our continual concealment of them. We make the Sophists: He

C. S. LEWIS

raises up a Socrates to answer them. Our third aim is, by these constructions, to destroy the devotional life. For the real presence of the Enemy, otherwise experienced by men in prayer and sacrament, we substitute a merely probable, remote, shadowy and uncouth figure, one who spoke a strange language and died a long time ago. Such an object cannot in fact be worshipped. Instead of the Creator adored by its creature, you soon have merely a leader acclaimed by a partisan, and finally a distinguished character approved by a judicious historian.

And fourthly, besides being un-historical in the Jesus it depicts, religion of this kind is false to history in another sense. No nation, and few individuals, are really brought into the Enemy's camp by the historical study of the biography of Jesus, simply as biography. . . . The earliest converts were converted by a single historical fact (the Resurrection) and a single theological doctrine (the Redemption) operating on a sense of sin which they already had—and sin, not against some new fancy-dress law produced as a novelty by a "great man," but against the old, platitudinous, universal moral law which they had been taught by their nurses and mothers.

The Screwtape Letters
Number 23

GOD AS MAN

Gᴏᴅ ᴄᴏᴜʟᴅ, had he pleased, have been incarnate in a man of iron nerves, the Stoic sort who lets no sigh escape him. Of His great humility He chose to be incarnate in a man of delicate sensibilities, who wept at the grave of Lazarus and sweated blood in Gethsemane. Otherwise we should have missed the great lesson that it is by his *will* alone that a man is good or bad, and that *feelings* are not, in themselves, of any importance. We should also have missed the all-important help of knowing that He has faced all that the weakest of us face, has shared not only the strength of our nature but every weakness of it except sin. If He had been incarnate in a man of immense natural courage, that would have been for many of us almost the same as His not being incarnate at all.

Letters of C. S. Lewis
23rd February 1947

COUNTING THE COST

A GOOD many people have been bothered by ...
Our Lord's words, "Be ye perfect." Some people seem to think this means "Unless you are perfect, I will not help you"; and as we cannot be perfect, then if He meant that, our position is hopeless. But I do not think He did mean that. I think He meant "The only help I will give is help to become perfect. You may want something less: but I will give you nothing less. . . . "

Now, if I may put it that way, Our Lord is like the dentists. If you give Him an inch, He will take an ell. Dozens of people go to Him to be cured of some one particular sin which they are ashamed of (like masturbation or physical cowardice) or which is obviously spoiling daily life (like bad temper or drunkenness). Well, He will cure it all right: but He will not stop there. That may be all you ask: but if once you call Him in, He will give you the full treatment.

That is why He warned people to "count the cost" before becoming Christians. "Make no mistake," He says, "if you let Me, I will make you perfect. The moment you put yourself in My hands, that is what you are in for. Nothing less, or other, than that. You have free will, and if you choose, you can push Me away. But if you do not push Me away, understand that I am going to see this job through. Whatever suffering it may cost you in your earthly life, whatever inconceivable purification it may cost you after death, whatever it costs Me, I will never rest nor let you rest until you are literally perfect—until My Father can say without reservation that He is well pleased with you, as He said He was well pleased with Me. This I can do and will do. But I will not do anything less."

Readings for Meditation and Reflection

And yet—this is the other and equally important side of it—this Helper who will, in the long run, be satisfied with nothing less than absolute perfection, will also be delighted with the first feeble, stumbling effort you make tomorrow to do the simplest duty. As a great Christian writer (George MacDonald) pointed out, every father is pleased at the baby's first attempt to walk: no father would be satisfied with anything less than a firm, free, manly walk in a grown-up son. In the same way, he said, "God is easy to please, but hard to satisfy."

Mere Christianity
Book IV Chapter 9

HALF-HEARTED CREATURES

IF YOU asked twenty good men today what they thought the highest of the virtues, nineteen of them would reply, Unselfishness. But if you had asked almost any of the great Christians of old, he would have replied, Love. You see what has happened? A negative term has been substituted for a positive, and this is of more than philological importance. The negative idea of Unselfishness carries with it the suggestion not primarily of securing good things for others, but of going without them ourselves, as if our abstinence and not their happiness was the important point. I do not think this is the Christian virtue of Love.

The New Testament has lots to say about self-denial, but not about self-denial as an end in itself. We are told to deny ourselves and to take up our crosses in order that we may follow Christ; and nearly every description of what we shall ultimately find if we do so contains an appeal to desire. If there lurks in most modern minds the notion that to desire our own good and earnestly to hope for the enjoyment of it is a bad thing, I submit that this notion has crept in from Kant and the Stoics, and is no part of the Christian faith.

Indeed, if we consider the unblushing promises of reward and the staggering nature of the rewards promised in the gospels, it would seem that Our Lord finds our desires, not too strong, but too weak. We are half-hearted creatures, fooling about with drink and sex and ambition when infinite joy is offered us, like an ignorant child who wants to go on making mud pies in a slum because he cannot imagine what is meant by the offer of a holiday at the sea. We are far too easily pleased.

Readings for Meditation and Reflection

We must not be troubled by unbelievers when they say that this promise of reward makes the Christian life a mercenary affair. There are different kinds of reward. There is the reward which has no natural connection with the things you do to earn it, and is quite foreign to the desires that ought to accompany those things. Money is not the natural reward of love, that is why we call a man mercenary if he marries a woman for the sake of her money. But marriage is the proper reward for a real lover, and he is not mercenary for desiring it. . . . The schoolboy beginning Greek grammar cannot look forward to his adult enjoyment of Sophocles as a lover looks forward to marriage or a General to victory. He has to begin by working for marks, or to escape punishment, or to please his parents, or, at best, in the hope of a future good which he cannot at present imagine or desire. His position, therefore, bears a certain resemblance to that of the mercenary; the reward he is going to get will, in actual fact, be a natural or proper reward, but he will not know that till he has got it. . . .

The Christian, in relation to heaven, is in much the same position as this schoolboy. Those who have attained everlasting life in the vision of God doubtless know very well that it is no mere bribe, but the very consummation of their earthly discipleship; but we who have not yet attained it cannot know this in the same way, and cannot even begin to know it at all except by continuing to obey and finding the first reward of our obedience in our increasing power to desire the ultimate reward.

"The Weight of Glory"
in *Screwtape Proposes a Toast*

C. S. LEWIS

TO BE LOVED BY GOD

In the end that Face which is the delight or the terror of the universe must be turned upon each of us either with one expression or with the other, either conferring glory inexpressible or inflicting shame that can never be cured or disguised. I read in a periodical the other day that the fundamental thing is how we think of God. By God Himself, it is not! How God thinks of us is not only more important, but infinitely more important. Indeed, how we think of Him is of no importance except insofar as it is related to how He thinks of us. It is written that we shall "stand before" Him, shall appear, shall be inspected. The promise of glory is the promise, almost incredible and only possible by the work of Christ, that some of us, that any of us who really chooses, shall actually survive that examination, shall find approval, shall please God. To please God . . . to be a real ingredient in the Divine happiness . . . to be loved by God, not merely pitied, but delighted in as an artist delights in his work or a father in a son—it seems impossible, a weight or burden of glory which our thoughts can hardly sustain. But so it is.

"The Weight of Glory"
in *Screwtape Proposes a Toast*

Readings for Meditation and Reflection

"ORDINARY" PEOPLE

I T IS a serious thing to live in a society of possible gods and goddesses, to remember that the dullest and most uninteresting person you can talk to may one day be a creature which, if you saw it now, you would be strongly tempted to worship, or else a horror and a corruption such as you now meet, if at all, only in a nightmare. All day long we are, in some degree, helping each other to one or other of these destinations. It is in the light of these overwhelming possibilities, it is with the awe and the circumspection proper to them, that we should conduct all our dealings with one another, all friendships, all loves, all play, all politics. There are no *ordinary* people. You have never talked to a mere mortal. Nations, cultures, arts, civilizations—these are mortal, and their life is to ours as the life of a gnat. But it is immortals whom we joke with, work with, marry, snub and exploit—immortal horrors or everlasting splendors. This does not mean that we are to be perpetually solemn. We must play. But our merriment must be of that kind (and it is, in fact, the merriest kind) which exists between people who have, from the outset, taken each other seriously—no flippancy, no superiority, no presumption. And our charity must be a real and costly love, with deep feeling for the sins in spite of which we love the sinner—no mere tolerance, or indulgence which parodies love as flippancy parodies merriment. Next to the Blessed Sacrament itself, your neighbor is the holiest object presented to your senses. If he is your Christian neighbor, he is holy in almost the same way, for in him also Christ *vere latitat*—the glorifier and the glorified, Glory Himself—is truly hidden.

"The Weight of Glory"
in *Screwtape Proposes a Toast*

C. S. LEWIS

BECOMING CLEAN MIRRORS

I N THE New Testament the art of life itself is an art of imitation: can we, believing this, believe that literature, which must derive from real life, is to aim at being "creative," "original," and "spontaneous"? "Originality" in the New Testament is quite plainly the prerogative of God alone; even within the triune being of God it seems to be confined to the Father. The duty and happiness of every other being is placed in being derivative, in reflecting like a mirror. Nothing could be more foreign to the tone of Scripture than the language of those who describe a saint as a "moral genius" or a "spiritual genius" thus insinuating that his virtue or spirituality is "creative" or "original."

If I have read the New Testament aright, it leaves no room for "creativeness" even in a modified or metaphorical sense. Our whole destiny seems to lie in the opposite direction, in being as little as possible ourselves, in acquiring a fragrance that is not our own but borrowed, in becoming clean mirrors filled with the image of a face that is not ours. I am not here supporting the doctrine of total depravity, and I do not say that the New Testament supports it; I am saying only that the highest good of a creature must be creaturely—that is, derivative or reflective—good. In other words, as St. Augustine makes plain . . . pride does not only go before a fall but is a fall—a fall of the creature's attention from what is better, God, to what is worse, itself. . . .

The unbeliever may take his own temperament and experience just as they happen to stand, and consider them worth communicating simply because they are facts or, worse still, because they are his. To the Christian his own temperament and experience, as mere fact, and as merely his, are of no value or importance whatsoever: he will deal with them, if at all, only because they are the medium through which, or the position from which, something universally profitable appeared to him.

We can imagine two men seated in different parts of a church or theater. Both, when they come out, may tell us their experiences, and both may use the first person. But the one is interested in his seat only because it was his—"I was most uncomfortable," he will say. "You would hardly believe what a draught comes in from the door in that corner. And the people! I had to speak pretty sharply to the woman in front of me." The other will tell us what could be seen from his seat, choosing to describe this because this is what he knows, and because every seat must give the best view of something. "Do you know," he will begin, "the molding on those pillars goes on round the back. It looks, too, as if the design on the back were the older of the two." Here we have the expressionist and the Christian attitudes towards the self or temperament.

"Christianity and Literature"
in *Christian Reflections*

C. S. LEWIS

SCREWTAPE ON
HELL'S IDEA OF HUMILITY

You MUST conceal from the patient the true end of Humility. Let him think of it not as self-forgetfulness but as a certain kind of opinion (namely, a low opinion) of his own talents and character. Some talents, I gather, he really has. Fix in his mind the idea that humility consists in trying to believe those talents to be less valuable than he believes them to be. No doubt they *are* in fact less valuable than he believes, but that is not the point. The great thing is to make him value an opinion for some quality other than truth, thus introducing an element of dishonesty and make-believe into the heart of what otherwise threatens to become a virtue. By this method thousands of humans have been brought to think that humility means pretty women trying to believe they are ugly, and clever men trying to believe they are fools. And since what they are trying to believe may, in some cases, be manifest nonsense, they cannot succeed in believing it and we have the chance of keeping their minds endlessly revolving on themselves in an effort to achieve the impossible.

To anticipate the Enemy's strategy, we must consider His aims. The Enemy wants to bring the man to a state of mind in which he could design the best cathedral in the world, and know it to be the best, and rejoice in the fact, without being any more (or less) or otherwise glad at having done it than he would be if it had been done by another. The Enemy wants him, in the end, to be so free from any bias in his own favor that he can rejoice in his own talents as frankly and gratefully as in his neighbor's talents—or in a sunrise, an elephant, or a waterfall. . . . His whole effort, therefore, will be to get the man's mind off the subject of his own value altogether. He would rather the man thought himself a great architect or a great poet and then forgot about it, than that he should spend much time and pains trying to think himself a bad one.

Your efforts to instill either vainglory or false modesty into the patient will therefore be met from the Enemy's side with the obvious reminder that a man is not usually called upon to have an opinion of his own talents at all, since he can very well go on improving them to the best of his ability without deciding on his precise niche in the temple of Fame.

The Screwtape Letters
Number 14

C. S. LEWIS

WE DELIGHT TO PRAISE

I THINK we delight to praise what we enjoy because the praise not merely expresses but completes the enjoyment; it is its appointed consummation. It is not out of compliment that lovers keep on telling one another how beautiful they are; the delight is incomplete till it is expressed. It is frustrating to have discovered a new author and not to be able to tell anyone how good he is; to come suddenly, at the turn of the road, upon some mountain valley of unexpected grandeur and then to have to keep silent because the people with you care for it no more than for a tin can in the ditch; to hear a good joke and find no one to share it with (the perfect hearer died a year ago). This is so even when our expressions are inadequate, as of course they usually are.

But how if one could really and fully praise even such things to perfection—utterly "get out" in poetry or music or paint the upsurge of appreciation which almost bursts you? Then indeed the object would be fully appreciated and our delight would have attained perfect development. The worthier the object, the more intense this delight would be. If it were possible for a created soul fully (I mean, up to the full measure conceivable in a finite being) to "appreciate," that is to love and delight in, the worthiest object of all, and simultaneously at every moment to give this delight perfect expression, then that soul would be in supreme beatitude.

It is along these lines that I find it easiest to understand the Christian doctrine that "Heaven" is a state in which angels now, and men hereafter, are perpetually employed in praising God. This does not mean, as it can so dismally suggest, that it is like "being in church." For our

"services" both in their conduct and in our power to partic-
ipate, are merely attempts at worship; never fully successful, often 99.9 per cent failures, sometimes total failures.
We are not riders but pupils in the riding school; for most
of us the falls and bruises, the aching muscles and the

severity of the exercise, far outweigh those few moments in
which we were, to our own astonishment, actually gallop-
ing without terror and without disaster.

To see what the doctrine really means, we must suppose ourselves to be in perfect love with God—drunk with,
drowned in, dissolved by, that delight which, far from remaining pent up within ourselves as incommunicable,
hence hardly tolerable, bliss, flows out from us incessantly
again in effortless and perfect expression, our joy no more
separable from the praise in which it liberates and utters itself than the brightness a mirror receives is separable from
the brightness it sheds. The Scotch catechism says that
man's chief end is "to glorify God and enjoy Him forever."
But we shall then know that these are the same thing.
Fully to enjoy is to glorify. In commanding us to glorify
Him, God is inviting us to enjoy Him.

Reflections on the Psalms
Chapter 9

C. S. LEWIS

WHY WE NEED A MAP

N A way I quite understand why some people are put off by Theology. I remember once when I had been giving a talk to the R.A.F., an old, hard-bitten officer got up and said, "I've no use for all that stuff. But, mind you, I'm a religious man too. I *know* there's a God. I've *felt* Him: out alone in the desert at night: the tremendous mystery. And that's just why I don't believe all your neat little dogmas and formulas about Him. To anyone who's met the real thing they all seem so petty and pedantic and unreal!"

Now in a sense I quite agreed with that man. I think he had probably had a real experience of God in the desert. And when he turned from that experience to the Christian creeds, I think he really was turning from something real to something less real. In the same way, if a man has once looked at the Atlantic from the beach, and then goes and looks at a map of the Atlantic, he also will be turning from something real to something less real: turning from real waves to a bit of colored paper. But here comes the point. The map is admittedly only colored paper, but there are two things you have to remember about it. In the first place, it is based on what hundreds and thousands of people have found out by sailing the real Atlantic. In that way it has behind it masses of experience just as real as the one you could have from the beach; only, while yours would be a single isolated glimpse, the map fits all those different experiences together. In the second place, if you want to go anywhere, the map is absolutely necessary. As long as you are content with walks on the beach, your own glimpses are far more fun than looking at a map. But the map is going to be more use than walks on the beach if you want to get to America.

Readings for Meditation and Reflection

Theology is like a map. Merely learning and thinking about the Christian doctrines, if you stop there, is less real and less exciting than the sort of thing my friend got in the desert. Doctrines are not God: they are only a kind of map. But that map is based on the experience of hundreds of people who really were in touch with God—experiences compared with which any thrills or pious feelings you and I are likely to get on our own are very elementary and very confused. And secondly, if you want to get any further, you must use the map. You see, what happened to that man in the desert may have been real, and was certainly exciting but nothing comes of it. It leads nowhere. There is nothing to do about it. In fact, that is just why a vague religion—all about feeling God in nature, and so on—is so attractive. It is all thrills and no work; like watching the waves from the beach. But you will not get to Newfoundland by studying the Atlantic that way, and you will not get eternal life by simply feeling the presence of God in flowers or music. Neither will you get anywhere by looking at maps without going to sea. Nor will you be very safe if you go to sea without a map.

In other words, Theology is practical: especially now. In the old days, when there was less education and discussion, perhaps it was possible to get on with a very few simple ideas about God. But it is not so now. Everyone reads, everyone hears things discussed. Consequently, if you do not listen to Theology, that will not mean that you have no ideas about God. It will mean that you have a lot of wrong ones—bad, muddled, out-of-date ideas. For a great many of the ideas about God which are trotted out as novelties today are simply the ones which real Theologians

C. S. LEWIS

tried centuries ago and rejected. To believe in the popular religion of modern England is retrogression—like believing the earth is flat.

Mere Christianity
Book IV Chapter 1

Readings for Meditation and Reflection

NATURAL LAW

EVERYONE has heard people quarreling. Sometimes it sounds funny and sometimes it sounds merely unpleasant; but however it sounds, I believe we can learn something very important from listening to the kind of things they say. They say things like this: "How'd you like it if anyone did the same to you?"—"That's my seat, I was there first"—"Leave him alone, he isn't doing you any harm"—"Why should you shove in first?"—"Give me a bit of your orange, I gave you a bit of mine"—"Come on, you promised." People say things like that every day, educated people as well as uneducated, and children as well as grown-ups.

Now what interests me about all these remarks is that the man who makes them is not merely saying that the other man's behavior does not happen to please him. He is appealing to some kind of standard of behavior which he expects the other man to know about. And the other man very seldom replies: "To hell with your standard." Nearly always he tries to make out that what he has been doing does not really go against the standard, or that if it does there is some special excuse. . . . It looks, in fact, very much as if both parties had in mind some kind of Law or Rule of fair play or decent behavior or morality or whatever you like to call it, about which they really agreed. And they have. If they had not, they might, of course, fight like animals, but they could not *quarrel* in the human sense of the word. Quarreling means trying to show that the other man is in the wrong. And there would be no sense in trying to do that unless you and he had some sort of agreement as to what Right and Wrong are; just as there would be no sense

C. S. LEWIS

in saying that a footballer had committed a foul unless there was some agreement about the rules of football. . . .

But the most remarkable thing is this. Whenever you find a man who says he does not believe in a real Right and Wrong, you will find the same man going back on this a moment later. He may break his promise to you, but if you try breaking one to him he will be complaining "It's not fair" before you can say Jack Robinson. A nation may say treaties do not matter; but then, next minute, they spoil their case by saying that the particular treaty they want to break was an unfair one. But if treaties do not matter, and if there is no such thing as Right and Wrong—in other words if there is no Law of Nature—what is the difference between a fair treaty and an unfair one? Have they not let the cat out of the bag and shown that whatever they say, they really know the Law of Nature just like anyone else?

It seems, then, we are forced to believe in a real Right and Wrong. People may be sometimes mistaken about them, just as people sometimes get their sums wrong, but they are not a matter of mere taste and opinion any more than the multiplication table. . . . These, then, are the two points I wanted to make. First, that human beings, all over the earth, have this curious idea that they ought to behave in a certain way, and cannot really get rid of it. Secondly, that they do not in fact behave in that way. They know the Law of Nature: they break it. These two facts are the foundation of all clear thinking about ourselves and the universe we live in.

Mere Christianity
Book 1 Chapter 1

MORALITY CANNOT
BECOME "STAGNANT"

THE MODERN mind has two lines of defense. The first claims that traditional morality is different in different times and places—in fact, that there is not one morality but a thousand. The second claims that to tie ourselves to an immutable moral code is to cut off all progress and acquiesce in "stagnation." Both are unsound.

Let us take the second one first. And let us strip it of the illegitimate emotional power it derives from the word "stagnation," with its suggestion of puddles and mantled pools. If water stands too long it stinks. To infer thence that whatever stands long must be unwholesome is to be the victim of metaphor. Space does not stink because it has preserved its three dimensions from the beginning. The square on the hypotenuse has not gone moldy by continuing to equal the sum of the squares on the other two sides. Love is not dishonored by constancy, and when we wash our hands we are seeking stagnation and "putting the clock back," artificially restoring our hands to the *status quo* in which they began the day and resisting the natural trend of events which would increase their dirtiness steadily from our birth to our death. For the emotive term "stagnant" let us substitute the descriptive term "permanent." Does a permanent moral standard preclude progress? On the contrary, except on the supposition of a changeless standard, progress is impossible. If good is a fixed point, it is at least possible that we should get nearer and nearer to it; but if the terminus is as mobile as the train, how can the train progress towards it? Our ideas of the good may change, but they cannot change either for the better or the worse if

C. S. LEWIS

there is no absolute and immutable good to which they can approximate or from which they can recede. We can go on getting a sum more and more nearly right only if the one perfectly right answer is "stagnant" . . .

And what of the second modern objection—that the ethical standards of different cultures differ so widely that there is no common tradition at all? The answer is that this is a lie—a good, solid, resounding lie. If a man will go into a library and spend a few days with the *Encyclopedia of Religion and Ethics* he will soon discover the massive unanimity of the practical reason in man. From the Babylonian *Hymn to Samos,* from the Laws of Manu, the *Book of the Dead,* the Analects, the Stoics, the Platonists, from Australian aborigines and Redskins, he will collect the same triumphantly monotonous denunciation of oppression, murder, treachery and falsehood, the same injunctions of kindness to the aged, the young, and the weak, of almsgiving and impartiality and honesty. . . . There are, of course, differences. There are even blindnesses in particular cultures—just as there are savages who cannot count up to twenty. But the pretense that we are presented with a mere chaos—that no outline of universally accepted value shows through—is simply false and should be contradicted in season and out of season whenever it is met. Far from finding a chaos, we find exactly what we should expect if good is indeed something objective and reason the organ whereby it is apprehended.

"The Poison of Subjectivism"
in *Christian Reflections*

Readings for Meditation and Reflection

LOOKING "ALONG"
AND LOOKING "AT"

I WAS standing today in the dark toolshed. The sun was shining outside and through the crack at the top of the door there came a sunbeam. From where I stood that beam of light, with the specks of dust floating in it, was the most striking thing in the place. Everything else was almost pitch black. I was seeing the beam, not seeing things by it.

Then I moved, so that the beam fell on my eyes. Instantly the whole previous picture vanished. I saw no tool shed, and (above all) no beam. Instead I saw, framed in the irregular cranny at the top of the door, green leaves moving on the branches of a tree outside and beyond, ninety-odd million miles away, the sun. Looking along the beam, and looking at the beam are very different experiences.

But this is only a very simple example of the differences between looking at and looking along. A young man meets a girl. The whole world looks different when he sees her. Her voice reminds him of something he has been trying to remember all his life, and ten minutes' casual chat with her is more precious than all the favors that all other women in the world could grant. He is, as they say, "in love." Now comes a scientist and describes this young man's experience from the outside. For him it is all an affair of the young man's genes and a recognized biological stimulus. That is the difference between looking *along* the sexual impulse and looking *at* it. . . .

You get one experience of a thing when you look along it and another when you look at it. Which is the "true" or "valid" experience? Which tells you most about

C. S. LEWIS

the thing? And you can hardly ask that question without noticing that for the last fifty years or so everyone has been taking the answer for granted. It has been assumed without discussion that if you want the true account of religion you must go, not to religious people, but to anthropologists; that if you want the true account of sexual love you must go, not to lovers, but to psychologists. . . .

The people who look *at* things have had it all their own way; the people who look *along* things have simply been brow-beaten. It has even come to be taken for granted that the external account of a thing somehow refutes or "debunks" the account given from inside. "All these moral ideals which look so transcendental and beautiful from inside," says the wiseacre, "are really only a mass of biological instincts and inherited taboos." And no one plays the game the other way round by replying, "If you will only step inside, the things that look to you like instincts and taboos will suddenly reveal their real and transcendental nature" . . .

The answer is that we must never allow the rot to begin. We must, on pain of idiocy, deny from the very outset the idea that looking *at* is, by its own nature, intrinsically truer or better than looking *along*. One must look both *along* and *at* everything.

"Meditation in a Toolshed"
in *First and Second Things*

BELIEF IN MIRACLES

IN ALL my life I have met only one person who claims to have seen a ghost. And the interesting thing about the story is that that person disbelieved in the immortal soul before she saw the ghost and still disbelieves after seeing it. She says that what she saw must have been an illusion or a trick of the nerves. And obviously she may be right. Seeing is not believing.

For this reason, the question whether miracles occur can never be answered simply by experience. Every event which might claim to be a miracle is, in the last resort, something presented to our senses, something seen, heard, touched, smelled or tasted. And our senses are not infallible. If anything extraordinary seems to have happened, we can always say that we have been the victims of an illusion. If we hold a philosophy which excludes the supernatural, this is what we always shall say. What we learn from experience depends on the kind of philosophy we bring to experience. It is therefore useless to appeal to experience before we have settled, as well as we can, the philosophical question.

If immediate experience cannot prove or disprove the miraculous, still less can history do so. Many people think one can decide whether a miracle occurred in the past by examining the evidence "according to the ordinary rules of historical inquiry." But the ordinary rules cannot be worked until we have decided whether miracles are possible, and if so, how probable they are. For if they are impossible, then no amount of historical evidence will convince us. If they are possible but immensely improbable, then only mathematically demonstrative evidence will convince us: and since history never provides that degree of evidence for any event, history can never convince us that a miracle occurred. If, on the other hand, miracles are not intrinsically improbable, then the existing evidence will be sufficient to convince us that quite a number of miracles have occurred. The result of our historical inquiries thus depends on the philosophical views which we have been holding before we even began to look at the evidence. The philosophical question must therefore come first.

Here is an example of the sort of thing that happens if we omit the preliminary philosophical task, and rush on to the historical. In a popular commentary on the Bible you will find a discussion of the date at which the Fourth Gospel was written. The author says it must have been written after the execution of St. Peter, because, in the Fourth Gospel, Christ is represented as predicting the execution of St. Peter. "A book," thinks the author, "cannot be written *before* events which it refers to." Of course it cannot—unless real predictions ever occur. If they do, then this argument for the date is in ruins. And the author has not discussed at all whether real predictions are possible. He takes it for granted (perhaps unconsciously) that they are not. Perhaps he is right: but if he is, he has not discovered this principle by historical inquiry. He has brought his disbelief in predictions to his historical work, so to speak, ready made. Unless he had done so his historical conclusion about the date of the Fourth Gospel could not have been reached at all. His work is therefore quite useless to a person who wants to know *whether* predictions occur. The author gets to work only after he has already answered that question in the negative, and on grounds which he never communicates to us.

Miracles
Chapter 1

A CAUTION
ABOUT METAPHORS

SOME people when they say that a thing is meant "metaphorically" conclude from this that it is hardly meant at all. They rightly think that Christ spoke metaphorically when he told us to carry the cross: they wrongly conclude that carrying the cross means nothing more that leading a respectable life and subscribing moderately to charities. They reasonably think that hell "fire" is a metaphor—and unwisely conclude that it means nothing more serious than remorse. They say that the story of the Fall in Genesis is not literal; and then go on to say (I have heard them myself) that it was really a fall upwards—which is like saying that because "My heart is broken" contains a metaphor, it therefore means "I feel very cheerful." This mode of interpretation I regard, frankly, as nonsense. For me the Christian doctrines which are "metaphorical"—or which have become metaphorical with the increase of abstract thought—mean something which is just as "supernatural" or shocking after we have removed the ancient imagery as it was before.

Miracles
Chapter 10

PRAYER

Some years ago I got up one morning intending to have my hair cut in preparation for a visit to London, and the first letter I opened made it clear I need not go to London. So I decided to put the haircut off too. But then there began the most unaccountable little nagging in my mind, almost like a voice saying, "Get it cut all the same. Go and get it cut." In the end I could stand it no longer. I went. Now my barber at that time was a fellow Christian and a man of many troubles whom my brother and I had sometimes been able to help. The moment I opened his shop door he said, "Oh, I was praying you might come today." And in fact if I had come a day or so later I should have been of no use to him.

It awed me; it awes me still. But of course one cannot rigorously prove a causal connection between the barber's prayers and my visit. It might be telepathy. It might be accident. . . .

The question then arises, "What sort of evidence would prove the efficacy of prayer?" The thing we pray for may happen, but how can you ever know it was not going to happen anyway? Even if the thing were indisputably miraculous it would not follow that the miracle had occurred because of your prayers. The answer surely is that a compulsive empirical proof such as we have in the sciences can never be attained.

Some things are proved by the unbroken uniformity of our experiences. The law of gravitation is established by the fact that, in our experience, all bodies without exception obey it. Now even if all the things that people prayed for happened, which they do not, this would not prove what Christians mean by the efficacy of prayer. For prayer is a request. The essence of request, as distinct from compulsion, is that it may or may not be granted. And if an infinitely wise Being listens to the requests of finite and foolish creatures, of course He will sometimes grant and sometimes refuse them.

"The Efficacy of Prayer"
in *Fern-seed and Elephants*

THE PRAYER
PRECEDING ALL PRAYERS

THE MOMENT of prayer is for me—or involves for me as its condition—the awareness, the re-awakened awareness, that this "real world" and "real self" are very far from being rock bottom realities. I cannot, in the flesh, leave the stage, either to go behind the scenes or to take my seat in the pit; but I can remember that these regions exist. And I also remember that my apparent self—this clown or hero or super—under his greasepaint is a real person with an offstage life. The dramatic person could not tread the stage unless he concealed a real person: unless the real and unknown I existed, I would not even make mistakes about the imagined one. And in prayer this real I struggle to speak, for once from his real being, and to address, for once, not the other actors, but—what shall I call Him? the Author, for He invented us all? The Producer, for He controls all? Or the Audience, for He watches, and will judge the performance?

The attempt is not to escape from space and time and from my creaturely situation as a subject facing objects. It is more modest: to re-awaken the awareness of that situation. If that can be done, there is no need to go anywhere else. This situation itself is, at every moment, a possible theophany. Here is the holy ground; the Bush is burning now.

Of course this attempt may be attended with almost every degree of success or failure. The prayer preceding all prayers is "May it be the real I who speaks. May it be the real Thou that I speak to." Infinitely various are the levels from which we pray. Emotional intensity is in itself no proof of spiritual depth. If we pray in terror we shall pray earnestly; it only proves that terror is an earnest emotion. Only God Himself can let the bucket down to the depths in us. And, on the other side, He must constantly work as the iconoclast. Every idea of Him we form, He must in mercy shatter. The most blessed result of prayer would be to rise thinking "But I never knew before. I never dreamed. . . ." I suppose it was at such a moment that Thomas Aquinas said of all his own theology, "It reminds me of straw."

Letters to Malcolm
Chapter 15

C. S. LEWIS

THE TROUBLE WITH "X"

WHEN we see how all our plans shipwreck on the characters of the people we have to deal with we are "in *one* way" seeing what it must be like for God. But only in one way. There are two respects in which God's view must be very different from ours. In the first place, He sees (like you) how all the people in your home or your job are in various degrees awkward or difficult; but when He looks into that home or factory or office He sees one more person of the same kind—the one you never do see. I mean, of course, yourself. That is the next great step in wisdom—to realize that you also are just that sort of person. You also have a fatal flaw in your character. All the hopes and plans of others have again and again shipwrecked on your character just as your hopes and plans have shipwrecked on theirs.

It is no good passing this over with some vague, general admission such as "Of course, I know I have my faults." It is important to realize that there is some really fatal flaw in you: something which gives the others just that same feeling of *despair* which their flaws give you. And it is almost certainly something you don't know about—like what the advertisements call "halitosis," which everyone notices except the person who has it. But why, you ask, don't the others tell me? Believe me, they have tried to tell you over and over again, and you just couldn't "take it." Perhaps a good deal of what you call their "nagging" or "bad temper" or "queerness" are just their attempts to make you see the truth. And even the faults you do know you don't know fully. You say, "I admit I lost my temper last night"; but the others know that you're always doing it, that you are a bad-tempered person. You say, "I admit I drank too much last Saturday"; but everyone else knows that you are an habitual drunkard. . . .

We don't like rationing which is imposed upon us, but I suggest one form of rationing which we ought to impose on ourselves. Abstain from all thinking about other people's faults, unless your duties as a teacher or parent make it necessary to think about them. Whenever the thoughts come unnecessarily into one's mind, why not simply shove them away? And think of one's own faults instead? For there, with God's help, one *can* do something. Of all the awkward people in your house or job there is only one whom you can improve very much. That is the practical end at which to begin. And really, we'd better. The job has to be tackled some day: and every day we put it off will make it harder to begin.

"The Trouble with 'X' "
in *God in the Dock*

FORGIVING AND EXCUSING

Forgiving does not mean excusing. Many people seem to think it does. They think that if you ask them to forgive someone who has cheated or bullied them you are trying to make out that there was really no cheating or no bullying. But if that were so, there would be nothing to forgive. They keep on replying, "But I tell you the man broke a most solemn promise." Exactly: that is precisely what you have to forgive. (This doesn't mean you must necessarily believe his next promise. It does mean that you must make every effort to kill every trace of resentment in your own heart—every wish to humiliate or hurt him or to pay him out.) The difference between this situation and the one in which you are asking God's forgiveness is this. In our own case we accept excuses too easily, in other people's we do not accept them easily enough. As regards my own sins it is a safe bet (though not a certainty) that the excuses are not really so good as I think: as regards other men's sins against me it is a safe bet (though not a certainty) that the excuses are better than I think. One must therefore begin by attending carefully to everything which may show that the other man was not so much to blame as we thought. But even if he is absolutely fully to blame we still have to forgive him; and even if 99 per cent of his apparent guilt can be explained away by really good excuses, the problem of forgiveness begins with the 1 per cent of guilt which is left over. To excuse what can really produce good excuses is not Christian charity; it is only fairness. To be a Christian means to forgive the inexcusable, because God has forgiven the inexcusable in you.

This is hard. It is perhaps not so hard to forgive a single great injury. But to forgive the incessant provocations of daily life—to keep on forgiving the bossy mother-in-law, the bullying husband, the nagging wife, the selfish daughter, the deceitful son—how can we do it? Only, I think, by remembering where we stand, by meaning our words when we say in our prayers each night "Forgive our trespasses as we forgive those that trespass against us." We are offered forgiveness on no other terms. To refuse it is to refuse God's mercy for ourselves. There is no hint of exceptions and God means what He says.

"On Forgiveness"
in *Fern-seed and Elephants*

C. S. LEWIS

CONFESSION

I T IS not for me to decide whether you should confess your sins to a priest or not ... but if you do
not, you should at least make a list on a piece of paper, and
make a serious act of penance about each one of them.
There is something about the mere words, you know, provided you avoid two dangers, either of sensational exaggeration—trying to work things up and make melodramatic
sins out of small matters—or the opposite danger of slur-
ring things over. It is essential to use the plain, simple, old-
fashioned words that you would use about anyone else. I
mean words like theft, or fornication, or hatred, instead of
"I did not mean to be dishonest," or "I was only a boy
then," or "I lost my temper." I think that this steady facing
of what one does know and bringing it before God, without excuses, and seriously asking for Forgiveness and
Grace, and resolving as far as in one lies to do better, is the
only way.

"Miserable Offenders"
in *Christian Reunion*

EMOTIONAL REACTION

In solitude, and also in confession, I have found (to my regret) that the degrees of shame and disgust which I actually feel at my own sins do not at all correspond to what my reason tells me about their comparative gravity. Just as the degree to which, in daily life, I feel the emotion of fear has very little to do with my rational judgment of the danger. I'd sooner have really nasty seas when I'm in an open boat than look down in perfect (actual) safety from the edge of a cliff. Similarly, I have confessed ghastly uncharities with less reluctance than small unmentionables—or those sins which happen to be ungentlemanly as well as un-Christian. Our emotional reactions to our own behavior are of limited ethical significance.

Letters to Malcolm
Chapter 18

C. S. LEWIS

GOD WANTS YOU
TO BE A SAINT

O F COURSE we never wanted, and never asked, to be made into the sort of creatures He is going to make us into. But the question is not what we intended ourselves to be, but what He intended us to be when He made us. He is the inventor, we are only the machine. He is the painter, we are only the picture. How should we know what He means us to be like? . . . We may be content to remain what we call "ordinary people": but He is determined to carry out a quite different plan. To shrink back from that plan is not humility: it is laziness and cowardice. To submit to it is not conceit or megalomania: it is obedience.

Here is another way of putting the two sides of the truth. On the one hand we must never imagine that our own unaided efforts can be relied on to carry us even through the next twenty-four hours as "decent" people. If He does not support us, not one of us is safe from some gross sin. On the other hand, no possible degree of holiness or heroism which has ever been recorded of the greatest saints is beyond what He is determined to produce in every one of us in the end. The job will not be completed in this life: but He means to get us as far as possible before death.

That is why we must not be surprised if we are in for a rough time. When a man turns to Christ and seems to be getting on pretty well (in the sense that some of his bad habits are now corrected), he often feels that it would now be natural if things went fairly smoothly. When troubles come along—illnesses, money troubles, new kinds of temptation—he is disappointed. These things, he feels, might have been necessary to rouse him and make him repent in his bad old days; but why now? Because God is forcing him on, or up, to a higher level: putting him into situations where he will have to be very much braver, or more patient, or more loving, than he ever dreamed of being before. It seems to us all unnecessary: but that is because we have not yet had the slightest notion of the tremendous thing He means to make of us. . . .

Imagine yourself as a living house. God comes in to rebuild that house. At first, perhaps, you can understand what He is doing. He is getting the drains right and stopping the leaks in the roof and so on: you knew that those jobs needed doing and so you are not surprised. But presently He starts knocking the house about in a way that hurts abominably and does not seem to make sense. What on earth is He up to? The explanation is that He is building quite a different house from the one you thought of—throwing out a new wing here, putting on an extra floor there, running up towers, making courtyards. You thought you were going to be made into a decent little cottage: but He is building a palace. He intends to come and live in it Himself.

Mere Christianity
Book IV Chapter 9

C. S. LEWIS

ENCORE!

I AM BEGINNING to feel that we need a preliminary act of submission not only towards possible future afflictions but also towards possible future blessings. I know it sounds fantastic; but think it over. It seems to me that we often, almost sulkily, reject the good that God offers us because, at that moment, we expected some other good. Do you know what I mean? On every level of our life—in our religious experience, in our gastronomic, erotic, aesthetic and social experience—we are always harking back to some occasion which seemed to us to reach perfection, setting that up as a norm, and depreciating all other occasions by comparison. But these other occasions, I now suspect, are often full of their own new blessing, if only we would lay ourselves open to it. God shows us a new facet of the glory, and we refuse to look at it because we're still looking for the old one. And of course we don't get that. You can't, at the twentieth reading, get again the experience of reading *Lycidas* for the first time. But what you do get can be in its own way as good.

This applies especially to the devotional life. Many religious people lament that the first fervours of their conversion have died away. They think—sometime rightly, but not, I believe, always—that their sins account for this. They may even try by pitiful efforts of will to revive what now seem to have been the golden days. But were those fervours—the operative word is *those*—ever intended to last?

It would be rash to say that there is any prayer which God *never* grants. But the strongest candidate is the prayer we might express in the single word *encore*. And how should the Infinite repeat Himself? All space and time are too little for Him to utter Himself in them *once*.

Readings for Meditation and Reflection

And the joke, or tragedy, of it all is that these golden moments in the past, which are so tormenting if we erect them into a norm, are entirely nourishing, wholesome and enchanting if we are content to accept them for what they are, for memories. Properly bedded down in a past which we do not miserably try to conjure back, they will send up exquisite growths. Leave the bulbs alone, and the new flowers will come up. Grub them up and hope, by fondling and sniffing, to get last year's blooms, and you will get nothing. "Unless a seed die . . . "

Letters to Malcolm
Chapter 5

C. S. LEWIS

THE NECESSITY OF PAIN

THE HUMAN spirit will not even begin to try to surrender self-will as long as all seems to be well with it. Now error and sin both have this property, that the deeper they are the less their victim suspects their existence; they are masked evil. Pain is unmasked, unmistakable evil, every man knows that something is wrong when he is being hurt.... And pain is not only immediately recognizable evil, but evil impossible to ignore. We can rest contentedly in our sins and in our stupidities; and anyone who has watched gluttons shoveling down the most exquisite foods as if they did not know what they were eating, will admit that we can ignore even pleasure. But pain insists upon being attended to. God whispers to us in our pleasures, speaks in our conscience, but shouts in our pains: it is His megaphone to rouse a deaf world....

I am progressing along the path of life in my ordinary contentedly fallen and godless condition, absorbed in a merry meeting with my friends for the morrow or a bit of work that tickles my vanity today, a holiday or a new book, when suddenly a stab of abdominal pain that threatens serious disease, or a headline in the newspapers that threatens us all with destruction, sends this whole pack of cards tumbling down. At first I am overwhelmed, and all my little happinesses look like broken toys. Then, slowly and reluctantly, bit by bit, I try to bring myself into the frame of mind that I should be in at all times. I remind myself that all these toys were never intended to possess my heart, that my true good is in another world, and my only real treasure is Christ. And perhaps, by God's grace, I succeed, and for a day or two become a creature consciously dependent on God and drawing its strength from the right sources.

Readings for Meditation and Reflection

But the moment the threat is withdrawn, my whole nature leaps back to the toys: I am even anxious, God forgive me, to banish from my mind the only thing that supported me under the threat because it is now associated with the misery of those few days. Thus the terrible necessity of tribulation is only too clear. God has had me for but forty-eight hours and then only by dint of taking everything else away from me. Let Him but sheathe that sword for a moment and I behave like a puppy when the hated bath is over—I shake myself as dry as I can and race off to reacquire my comfortable dirtiness, if not in the nearest manure heap, at least in the nearest flower bed. And that is why tribulations cannot cease until God either sees us remade or sees that our remaking is now hopeless.

The Problem of Pain
Chapter 6

C. S. LEWIS

MISFORTUNE

W<small>E ARE</small> perplexed to see misfortune falling upon decent, inoffensive, worthy people—on capable, hard-working mothers of families or diligent, thrifty, little trades people, on those who have worked so hard, and so honestly, for their modest stock of happiness and now seem to be entering on the enjoyment of it with the fullest right. How can I say with sufficient tenderness what here needs to be said? It does not matter that I know I must become, in the eyes of every hostile reader, as it were personally responsible for all the sufferings I try to explain— just as, to this day, everyone talks as if St. Augustine *wanted* unbaptized infants to go to Hell. But it matters enormously if I alienate anyone from the truth.

Let me implore the reader to try to believe, if only for the moment, that God, who made these deserving people, may really be right when He thinks that their modest prosperity and the happiness of their children are not enough to make them blessed: that all this must fall from them in the end, and that if they have not learned to know Him they will be wretched. And therefore He troubles them, warning them in advance of an insufficiency that one day they will have to discover. The life to themselves and their families stands between them and the recognition of their need; He makes that life less sweet to them. I call this a Divine humility because it is a poor thing to strike our colors to God when the ship is going down under us; a poor thing to come to Him as a last resort, to offer up "our own" when it is no longer worth keeping. If God were proud He would hardly have us on such terms: but He is not proud, He stoops to conquer, He will have us even

though we have shown that we prefer everything else to
Him, and come to Him because there is "nothing better"
now to be had.

The Problem of Pain
Chapter 6

C. S. LEWIS

THE DIVORCE OF
HEAVEN AND HELL

Blake wrote the *Marriage of Heaven and Hell*....
In some sense or other the attempt to make that
marriage is perennial. The attempt is based on the belief
that reality never presents us with an absolutely unavoidable "either-or"; that, granted skill and patience and (above
all) time enough, some way of embracing both alternatives
can always be found; that mere development or adjustment
or refinement will somehow turn evil into good without
our being called on for a final and total rejection of anything we should like to retain.

This belief I take to be a disastrous error. You cannot
take all luggage with you on all journeys; on one journey
even your right hand and your right eye may be among the
things you have to leave behind. We are not living in a
world where all roads are radii of a circle and where all, if
followed long enough, will therefore draw gradually
nearer and finally meet at the center: rather in a world
where every road, after a few miles forks into two, and
each of those into two again, and at each fork you must
make a decision. Even on the biological level life is not like
a pool but like a tree. It does not move towards unity but
away from it, and the creatures grow further apart as they
increase in perfection. Good, as it ripens, becomes continually more different not only from evil but from other good.

I do not think that all who choose wrong roads per-
ish; but their rescue consists in being put back on the right
road. A wrong sum can be put right: but only by going
back till you find the error and working it afresh from that
point, never by simply *going on*. Evil can be undone, but it
cannot "develop" into good. Time does not heal it. The

spell must be unwound, bit by bit, "with backward mutters of dissevering power"—or else not. It is still "either-or." If we insist on keeping Hell (or even earth) we shall not see Heaven: if we accept Heaven we shall not be able to retain even the smallest and most intimate souvenirs of Hell. I believe, to be sure, that any man who reaches Heaven will find that what he abandoned (even in plucking out his right eye) was precisely nothing: that the kernel of what he was really seeking even in his most depraved wishes will be there, beyond expectation, waiting for him in "the High Countries." In that sense it will be true for those who have completed the journey (and for no others) to say that good is everything and Heaven everywhere. But we, at this end of the road, must not try to anticipate that retrospective vision. If we do, we are likely to embrace the false and disastrous converse and fancy that everything is good and everywhere is Heaven.

But what, you ask, of earth? Earth, I think, will not be found by anyone to be in the end a very distinct place. I think earth, if chosen instead of Heaven, will turn out to have been, all along, only a region in Hell: and earth, if put second to Heaven, to have been from the beginning a part of Heaven itself.

Preface to *The Great Divorce*

C. S. LEWIS

HOPE

MOST of us find it very difficult to want "Heaven" at all—except in so far as "Heaven" means meeting again our friends who have died. One reason for this difficulty is that we have not been trained: our whole education tends to fix our minds on this world. Another reason is that when the real want for Heaven is present in us, we do not recognize it. Most people, if they had really learned to look into their own hearts, would know that they do want, and want acutely, something that cannot be had in this world. There are all sorts of things in this world that offer to give it to you, but they never quite keep their promise. The longings which arise in us when we first fall in love, or first think of some foreign country, or first take up some subject that excites us, are longings which no marriage, no travel, no learning, can really satisfy. I am not now speaking of what would be ordinarily called unsuccessful marriages, or holidays, or learned careers. I am speaking of the best possible ones. There was something we grasped at, in that first moment of longing, which just fades away in the reality. I think everyone knows what I mean. The wife may be a good wife, and the hotels and scenery may have been excellent, and chemistry may be a very interesting job: but something has evaded us. Now there are two wrong ways of dealing with this fact, and one right one.

1 The Fool's Way.—He puts the blame on the things themselves. He goes on all his life thinking that if only he tried another woman, or went for a more expensive holiday, or whatever it is, then, this time, he really would catch the mysterious something we are all after. . . .

Readings for Meditation and Reflection

2   The Way of the Disillusioned "Sensible Man."—
He soon decides that the whole thing was moonshine. "Of
course," he says, "one feels like that when one's young. But
by the time you get to my age you've given up chasing the
rainbow's end." And so he settles down and learns not to
expect too much, and represses the part of himself which
used, as he would say, "to cry for the moon . . . "

3   The Christian Way.—The Christian says,
"Creatures are not born with desires unless satisfaction for
those desires exists. A baby feels hunger: well, there is such
a thing as food. A duckling wants to swim: well, there is
such a thing as water. Men feel sexual desire: well, there is
such a thing as sex. If I find in myself a desire which no experience in this world can satisfy, the most probable explanation is that I was made for another world. If none of my
earthly pleasures satisfy it, that does not prove that the universe is a fraud. Probably earthly pleasures were never
meant to satisfy it, but only to arouse it, to suggest the real
thing. If that is so, I must take care, on the one hand, never
to despise, or be unthankful for, these earthly blessings, and
on the other, never to mistake them for the something else
of which they are only a kind of copy, or echo, or mirage. I
must keep alive in myself the desire for my true country,
which I shall not find till after death; I must never let it get
snowed under or turned aside; I must make it the main object of life to press on to that other country and to help others to do the same."

Mere Christianity
Book iii Chapter 10

C. S. LEWIS

THE GREAT SIN

THERE is one vice of which no man in the world is free; which every one in the world loathes when he sees it in someone else; and of which hardly any people, except Christians, ever imagine that they are guilty themselves. I have heard people admit that they are bad-tempered, or that they cannot keep their heads about girls or drink, or even that they are cowards. I do not think I have ever heard anyone who was not a Christian accuse himself of this vice. . . ..

The vice I am talking of is Pride or Self-Conceit: and the virtue opposite to it, in Christian morals, is called Humility. . . . According to Christian teachers, the essential vice, the utmost evil, is Pride. Unchastity, anger, greed, drunkenness, and all that, are mere flea bites in comparison: it was through Pride that the devil became the devil: Pride leads to every other vice: it is the complete anti-God state of mind.

Does this seem to you exaggerated? If so, think it over. I pointed out a moment ago that the more pride one had, the more one disliked pride in others. In fact, if you want to find out how proud you are the easiest way is to ask yourself, "How much do I dislike it when other people snub me, or refuse to take any notice of me, or shove their oar in, or patronize me, or show off?" The point is that each person's pride is in competition with everyone else's pride. It is because I wanted to be the big noise at the party that I am so annoyed at someone else being the big noise. Two of a trade never agree. Now what you want to get clear is that Pride is *essentially* competitive—is competitive by its very nature—while the other vices are competitive only, so to speak, by accident. Pride gets no pleasure out of having something, only out of having more of it than the next man. We say that people are proud of being rich, or clever, or good-looking, but they are not. They are proud of being richer, or cleverer, or better-looking than others. If every one else became equally rich, or clever, or good-looking there would be nothing to be proud about. It is the comparison that makes you proud: the pleasure of being above the rest. . . .

The Christians are right: it is Pride which has been the chief cause of misery in every nation and every family since the world began. Other vices may sometimes bring people together: you may find good fellowship and jokes and friendliness among drunken people or unchaste people. But Pride always means enmity—it *is* enmity. And not only enmity between man and man, but enmity to God.

In God you come up against something which is in every respect immeasurably superior to yourself. Unless you know God as that—and, therefore, know yourself as nothing in comparison—you do not know God at all. As long as you are proud you cannot know God. A proud man is always looking down on things and people: and, of course, as long as you are looking down, you cannot see something that is above you. . . .

It is a terrible thing that the worst of all the vices can smuggle itself into the very center of our religious life. But you can see why. The other, and less bad, vices come from the devil working on us through our animal nature. But this does not come through our animal nature at all. It comes direct from Hell. It is purely spiritual: consequently it is far more subtle and deadly. For the same reason, Pride can often be used to beat down the simpler vices. Teachers, in fact, often appeal to a boy's Pride, or, as they call it, his self-respect, to make him behave decently: many a man has

C. S. LEWIS

overcome cowardice, or lust, or ill-temper, by learning to
think that they are beneath his dignity—that is, by Pride.
The devil laughs. He is perfectly content to see you becoming chaste and brave and self-controlled provided, all the
time, he is setting up in you the Dictatorship of Pride—just
as he would be quite content to see your chilblains cured if
he was allowed, in return, to give you cancer. For Pride is
spiritual cancer: it eats up the very possibility of love, or
contentment, or even common sense.

Mere Christianity
Book III Chapter 8

SCREWTAPE ON WORLDLINESS

Prosperity knits a man to the World. He feels that he is "finding his place in it," while really it is finding its place in him. His increasing reputation, his widening circle of acquaintances, his sense of importance, the growing pressure of absorbing and agreeable work, build up in him a sense of being really at home in earth which is just what we want. You will notice that the young are generally less unwilling to die than the middle-aged and the old.

The truth is that the Enemy, having oddly destined these mere animals to life in His own eternal world, has guarded them pretty effectively from the danger of feeling at home anywhere else. That is why we must often wish long life to our patients; seventy years is not a day too much for the difficult task of unraveling their souls from Heaven and building up a firm attachment to the earth. While they are young we find them always shooting off at a tangent. Even if we contrive to keep them ignorant of explicit religion, the incalculable winds of fantasy and music and poetry—the mere face of a girl, the song of a bird, or the sight of a horizon—are always blowing our whole structure away. They *will* not apply themselves steadily to worldly advancement, prudent connections, and the policy of safety first. So inveterate is their appetite for Heaven that our best method, at this stage, of attaching them to earth is to make them believe that earth can be turned into Heaven at some future date by politics or eugenics or "science" or psychology, or what not. Real worldliness is a work of time—assisted, of course by pride, for we teach them to describe the creeping death as good sense or Maturity or Experience. . . .

C. S. LEWIS

How valuable time is to us may be gauged by the fact that the Enemy allows us so little of it. The majority of the human race dies in infancy; of the survivors, a good many die in youth. It is obvious that to Him human birth is important chiefly as the qualification for human death, and death solely as the gate to that other kind of life.

The Screwtape Letters
Number 28

Readings for Meditation and Reflection

SEXUAL MORALITY

THEY tell you sex has become a mess because it was hushed up. But for the last twenty years it has not been hushed up. It has been chattered about all day long. Yet it is still in a mess. If hushing up had been the cause of the trouble, ventilation would have set it right. But it has not. I think it is the other way round. I think the human race originally hushed it up because it had become such a mess. Modern people are always saying, "Sex is nothing to be ashamed of." They may mean two things. They may mean "There is nothing to be ashamed of in the fact that the human race reproduces itself in a certain way, nor in the fact that it gives pleasure." If they mean that, they are right. Christianity says the same. It is not the thing, nor the pleasure, that is the trouble. The old Christian teachers said that if man had never fallen, sexual pleasure, instead of being less than it is now, would actually have been greater. I know some muddle-headed Christians have talked as if Christianity thought that sex, or the body, or pleasure, were bad in themselves. But they were wrong. Christianity is almost the only one of the great religions which thoroughly approves of the body—which believes that matter is good, that God Himself once took on a human body, that some kind of body is going to be given to us even in Heaven and is going to be an essential part of our happiness, our beauty and our energy. Christianity has glorified marriage more than any other religion: and nearly all the greatest love poetry in the world has been produced by Christians. If anyone says that sex, in itself, is bad, Christianity contradicts him at once. But, of course, when people say, "Sex is nothing to be ashamed of," they may mean "the state into which the sexual instinct has now got is nothing to be ashamed of."

If they mean that, I think they are wrong. I think it is everything to be ashamed of. There is nothing to be ashamed of in enjoying your food: there would be everything to be ashamed of if half the world made food the main interest of their lives and spent their time looking at pictures of food and dribbling and smacking their lips. I do not say you and I are individually responsible for the present situation. Our ancestors have handed over to us organisms which are warped in this respect: and we grow up surrounded by propaganda in favor of unchastity. There are people who want to keep our sex instinct inflamed in order to make money out of us. Because, of course, a man with an obsession is a man who has very little sales-resistance. God knows our situation; He will not judge us as if we had no difficulties to overcome. What matters is the sincerity and perseverance of our will to overcome them.

Mere Christianity
Book III Chapter 5

SCREWTAPE ON
HELL'S VIEW OF PLEASURE

NEVER forget that when we are dealing with any pleasure in its healthy and normal and satisfying form, we are, in a sense, on the Enemy's ground. I know we have won many a soul through pleasure. All the same, it is His invention, not ours. He made the pleasures: all our research so far has not enabled us to produce one. All we can do is to encourage the humans to take the pleasures which our Enemy has produced, at times, or in ways, or in degrees, which He has forbidden. Hence we always try to work away from the natural condition of any pleasure to that in which it is least natural, least redolent of its Maker, and least pleasurable. An ever-increasing craving for an ever-diminishing pleasure is the formula. It is more certain; and it's better *style*. To get the man's soul and give him *nothing* in return—that is what really gladdens our Father's heart.

The Screwtape Letters
Number 9

C. S. LEWIS

WE HAVE NO
"RIGHT TO HAPPINESS"

"AFTER ALL," said Clare, "they had a right to
happiness."

We were discussing something that once happened in
our own neighborhood. Mr. A. had deserted Mrs. A. and got
his divorce in order to marry Mrs. B., who had likewise got
her divorce in order to marry Mr. A. And there was certainly no doubt that Mr. A. and Mrs. B. were very much in
love . . . and if nothing went wrong with their health or their
income, they might reasonably expect to be very happy.

It was equally clear that they were not happy with
their old partners. Mrs. B. had adored her husband at the
outset. But then he got smashed up in the war. It was
thought he had lost his virility, and it was known that he
had lost his job. Life with him was no longer what Mrs. B.
had bargained for. Poor Mrs. A., too. She had lost her
looks—and all her liveliness. It might be true, as some said,
that she consumed herself by bearing his children and
nursing him through the long illness that overshadowed
their earlier married life. . . . Her suicide was a terrible
shock to him. We all knew this, for he told us so himself.
"But what could I do?," he said. "A man has a right to happiness. I had to take my own chance when it came" . . .

It is part of the nature of a strong erotic passion—as
distinct from a transient fit of appetite—that it makes
more towering promises than any other emotion. No doubt
all our desires make promises, but not so impressively. To
be in love involves the most irresistible conviction that one
will go on being in love until one dies, and that possession
of the beloved will confer, not merely frequent ecstasies,
but settled, fruitful, deep-rooted, lifelong happiness. Hence

all seems to be at stake. If we miss this chance we shall have lived in vain. At the very thought of such a doom we sink into fathomless depths of self-pity. . . .

If we establish a "right to (sexual) happiness" which supersedes all the ordinary rules of behavior, we do so not because of what our passion shows itself to be in experience but because of what it professes to be while we are in the grip of it. Hence, while the bad behavior is real and works miseries and degradations, the happiness which was the object of the behavior turns out again and again to be illusory. Everyone (except Mr. A. and Mrs. B.) knows that Mr. A. in a year or so may have the same reason for deserting his new wife as for deserting his old. He will feel again that all is at stake. He will see himself again as the great lover, and his pity for himself will exclude all pity for the woman. . . .

A society in which conjugal infidelity is tolerated must always be in the long run a society adverse to women. Women, whatever a few male songs and satires may say to the contrary, are more naturally monogamous than men; it is a biological necessity. Where promiscuity prevails, they will therefore always be more often the victims than the culprits. Also, domestic happiness is more necessary to them than to us. And the quality by which they most easily hold a man, their beauty, decreases every year after they have come to maturity, but this does not happen to those qualities of personality—women don't really care tuppence about our *looks*—by which we hold women. Thus in the ruthless war of promiscuity women are at a double disadvantage. They play for higher stakes and are also more likely to lose. I have no sympathy with moralists who frown at the increasing crudity of female

C. S. LEWIS

provocativeness. These signs of desperate competition fill me with pity. . . .

Though the "right to happiness" is chiefly claimed for the sexual impulse, it seems to me impossible that the matter should stay there. The fatal principle, once allowed in that department, must sooner or later seep through our whole lives. We thus advance towards a state of society in which not only each man but every impulse in each man claims *carte blanche*. And then, though our technological skill may help us survive a little longer, our civilization will have died at heart, and will—one dare not even add "unfortunately"—be swept away.

"We have no 'Right to Happiness'"
in *God in the Dock*

LIKING AND LOVING

Though natural likings should normally be encouraged, it would be quite wrong to think that the way to become charitable is to sit trying to manufacture affectionate feelings. Some people are "cold" by temperament; that may be a misfortune for them, but it is no more a sin than having a bad digestion is a sin; and it does not cut them out from the chance, or excuse them from the duty, of learning charity.

The rule for all of us is perfectly simple. Do not waste time bothering whether you "love" your neighbor; act as if you did. As soon as we do this we find one of the great secrets. When you are behaving as if you loved someone, you will presently come to love him. If you injure someone you dislike, you will find yourself disliking him more. If you do him a good turn, you will find yourself disliking him less.

There is, indeed, one exception. If you do him a good turn, not to please God and obey the law of charity, but to show him what a fine forgiving chap you are, and to put him in your debt, and then sit down to wait for his "gratitude," you will probably be disappointed. (People are not fools: they have a very quick eye for anything like showing off, or patronage.) But whenever we do good to another self, just because it is a self, made (like us) by God, and desiring its own happiness as we desire ours, we shall have learned to love it a little more or, at least, to dislike it less.

Consequently, though Christian charity sounds a very cold thing to people whose heads are full of sentimentality, and though it is quite distinct from affection, yet it leads to affection. The difference between a Christian and a worldly man is not that the worldly man has only affections or "likings" and the Christian has only "charity." The worldly man treats certain people kindly because he "likes" them: the Christian, trying to treat everyone kindly, finds himself liking more and more people as he goes on—including people he could not even have imagined himself liking at the beginning . . .

Some writers use the word charity to describe not only Christian love between human beings, but also God's love for man and man's love for God. About the second of these two, people are often worried. They are told they ought to love God. They cannot find any such feelings in themselves. What are they to do? The answer is the same as before. Act as if you did. Do not sit trying to manufacture feelings. Ask yourself, "If I were sure that I loved God, what would I do?" When you have found the answer, go and do it.

Mere Christianity
Book III Chapter 9

ON PRAYING

No one in his senses, if he has any power of or-
dering his own day, would reserve his chief
prayers for bed-time—obviously the worst possible hour
for any action which needs concentration. The trouble is
that thousands of unfortunate people can hardly find any
other. Even for us, who are the lucky ones, it is not always
easy. My own plan, when hard pressed, is to seize any time,
and place, however unsuitable, in preference to the last
waking moment. On a day of traveling—with, perhaps,
some ghastly meeting at the end of it—I'd rather pray sitting in a crowded train than put it off till midnight when
one reaches a hotel bedroom with aching head and dry
throat, and one's mind partly in a stupor and partly in a
whirl. On other, and slightly less crowded, days a bench in
a park, or a back street where one can pace up and down,
will do.

A man to whom I was explaining this said, "But
why don't you turn into a church?" Partly because, for nine
months of the year, it will be freezingly cold, but also because I have had bad luck with churches. No sooner do I
enter one and compose my mind than one or other of two
things happens. Either someone starts practicing the organ.
Or else, with resolute tread, there appears from nowhere a
pious woman in elastic side-boots, carrying mop, bucket,
and dust-pan, and begins beating hassocks and rolling up
carpets and doing things to flower vases. Of course (blessings on her) "work is prayer," and her enacted *oratio* is
probably worth ten times my spoken one. But it doesn't
help mine to become worth more.

When one prays in strange places and at strange
times one can't kneel, to be sure. I won't say this doesn't

matter. The body ought to pray as well as the soul. Body and soul are both the better for it. Bless the body. Mine has led me into many scrapes, but I've led it into far more. If the imagination were obedient, the appetites would give us very little trouble. And from how much it has saved me! And but for our body one whole realm of God's glory—all that we receive through the senses—would go unpraised. For the beasts can't appreciate it and the angels are, I suppose, pure intelligences. They *understand* colors and tastes better than our greatest scientists; but have they retinas or palates? I fancy the "beauties of nature" are a secret God has shared with us alone. That may be one of the reasons why we were made—and why the resurrection of the body is an important doctrine.

But I'm being led into a digression. . . . The relevant point is that kneeling does matter, but other things matter even more. A concentrated mind and a sitting body make for better prayer than a kneeling body and a mind half asleep. Sometimes these are the only alternatives. . . .

A clergyman once said to me that a railway compartment, if one has it to oneself, is an extremely good place to pray in "because there is just the right amount of distraction." When I asked him to explain, he said that perfect silence and solitude left one more open to the distractions which come from within, and that a moderate amount of external distraction was easier to cope with. I don't find this so myself, but I can imagine it.

Letters to Malcolm
Chapter 3

Readings for Meditation and Reflection

READY-MADE PRAYERS

For many years after my conversion I never used any ready-made forms except the Lord's Prayer. In fact I tried to pray without words at all—not to verbalize the mental acts. Even in praying for others I believe I tended to avoid their names and substituted mental images of them. I still think the prayer without words is the best—if one can really achieve it. But I now see that in trying to make it my daily bread I was counting on a greater mental and spiritual strength than I really have. To pray successfully without words one needs to be "at the top of one's form." Otherwise the mental acts become merely imaginative or emotional acts—and a fabricated emotion is a miserable affair. When the golden moments come, when God enables one really to pray without words, who but a fool would reject the gift? But He does not give it—anyway not to me—day in, day out. My mistake was what Pascal, if I remember rightly, calls "Error of Stoicism": thinking we can do always what we can do sometimes. . . .

For me words are . . . secondary. They are only an anchor. Or, shall I say, they are the movements of a conductor's baton: not the music. They serve to canalize the worship or penitence or petition which might without them—such are our minds—spread into wide and shallow puddles. It does not matter very much who first put them together. If they are our own words they will soon, by unavoidable repetition, harden into a formula. If they are someone else's, we shall continually pour into them our own meaning. . . .

I need not stress the importance of the home-made staple. As Solomon said at the dedication of the temple, each man who prays knows "the plague of his own heart."

C. S. LEWIS

Also, the comforts of his own heart. No other creature is identical with me; no other situation identical with mine . . . . This is obvious.

Perhaps I shan't find it easy to persuade you that the ready-made modicum has also its use: for me, I mean—I'm not suggesting rules for anyone else in the whole world.

First, it keeps me in touch with "sound doctrine." Left to oneself, one could easily slide away from "the faith once given" into a phantom called "my religion."

Secondly, it reminds me "what things I ought to ask" (perhaps especially when I am praying for other people). The crisis of the present moment, like the nearest telegraph post, will always loom largest. Isn't there a danger that our great, permanent, objective necessities—often more important—may get crowded out?

Letters to Malcolm
Chapter 2

PRAYER AND TIME

I SHOULD like to deal with a difficulty that some people find about the whole idea of prayer. A man put it to me by saying "I can believe in God all right, but what I cannot swallow is the idea of Him attending to several hundred million human beings who are all addressing Him at the same moment." And I have found that quite a lot of people feel this.

Now, the first thing to notice is that the whole sting of it comes in the words *at the same moment.* Most of us can imagine God attending to any number of applicants if only they came one by one and He had an endless time to do it in. So what is really at the back of this difficulty is the idea of God having to fit too many things into one moment of time.

Well that is of course what happens to us. Our life comes to us moment by moment. One moment disappears before the next comes along: and there is room for very little in each. That is what Time is like. And of course you and I tend to take it for granted that this Time series—this arrangement of past, present and future—is not simply the way life comes to us but the way all things really exist. We tend to assume that the whole universe and God Himself are always moving on from past to future just as we do. But many learned men do not agree with that. It was the Theologians who first started the idea that some things are not in Time at all: later the philosophers took it over and now some of the scientists are doing the same.

Almost certainly God is not in Time. His life does not consist of moments following one another. If a million people are praying to Him at ten-thirty tonight, He need not listen to them all in that one little snippet which we call ten-thirty. Ten-thirty—and every other moment from the beginning of the world—is always the Present for Him. If you like to put it that way, He has all eternity in which to listen to the split second of prayer put up by a pilot as his plane crashes in flames.

That is difficult, I know. Let me try to give some-thing, not the same, but a bit like it. Suppose I am writing a novel. I write, "Mary laid down her work; next moment came a knock at the door!" For Mary who has to live in the imaginary time of my story there is no interval between putting down the work and hearing the knock. But I, who am Mary's maker, do not live in the imaginary time at all. Between writing the first half of that sentence and the second, I might sit down for three hours and think steadily about Mary. I could think about Mary as if she were the only character in the book and for as long as I pleased, and the hours I spent in doing so would not appear in Mary's time (the time inside the story) at all.

This is not a perfect illustration, of course. But it may give just a glimpse of what I believe to be the truth. God is not hurried along in the Time-stream of this universe any more than an author is hurried along in the imaginary time of his own novel. He has infinite attention to spare for each one of us. He does not have to deal with us in the mass. You are as much alone with Him as if you were the only being He had ever created. When Christ died, He died for you individually just as much as if you had been the only man in the world.

Mere Christianity
Book IV Chapter 3

Readings for Meditation and Reflection

SCREWTAPE ON TIME

MEN ARE not angered by mere misfortune but by misfortune conceived as injury. And the sense of injury depends on the feeling that a legitimate claim has been denied. The more claims on life, therefore, that your patient can be induced to make, the more often he will feel injured and, as a result, ill-tempered. Now you will have noticed that nothing throws him into a passion so easily as to find a tract of time which he reckoned on having at his own disposal unexpectedly taken from him. It is the unexpected visitor (when he looked forward to a quiet evening), or the friend's talkative wife (turning up when he looked forward to a *tête-à-tête* with the friend), that throw him out of gear. Now he is not yet so uncharitable or slothful that these small demands on his courtesy are *in themselves* too much for it. They anger him because he regards his time as his own and feels that it is being stolen. You must therefore zealously guard in his mind the curious assumption "My time is my own." Let him have the feeling that he starts each day as the lawful possessor of twenty-four hours. Let him feel as a grievous tax that portion of this property which he has to make over to his employers, and as a generous donation that further portion which he allows to religious duties. But what he must never be permitted to doubt is that the total from which these deductions have been made was, in some mysterious sense, his own personal birthright.

You have here a delicate task. The assumption which you want him to go on making is so absurd that, if once it is questioned, even we cannot find a shred of argument in its defense. The man can neither make, nor retain, one moment of time; it all comes to him by pure gift; he might as well regard the sun and moon as his chattels. He is also, in theory, committed to a total service of the Enemy; and if the Enemy appeared to him in bodily form and demanded that total service for even one day, he would not refuse. He would be greatly relieved if that one day involved nothing harder than listening to the conversation of a foolish woman; and he would be relieved almost to the pitch of disappointment if for one half-hour in that day the Enemy said "Now you go and amuse yourself." Now if he thinks about his assumption for a moment, even he is bound to realize that he is actually in this situation every day.

The Screwtape Letters
Number 21

SCREWTAPE GIVES HELL'S VIEW OF THE PRESENT

THE HUMANS live in time but our Enemy destines them to eternity. He, therefore, I believe, wants them to attend chiefly to two things, to eternity itself, and to that point of time which they call the Present. For the Present is the point at which time touches eternity. Of the present moment, and of it only, humans have an experience analogous to the experience which our Enemy has of reality as a whole; in it alone freedom and actuality are offered them. He would therefore have them continually concerned either with eternity (which means being concerned with Him) or with the Present—either meditating on their eternal union with, or separation from, Himself, or else obeying the present voice of conscience, giving thanks for the present pleasure. . . .

To be sure, the Enemy wants men to think of the Future too—just so much as is necessary for *now* planning the acts of justice or charity which will probably be their duty tomorrow. The duty of planning the morrow's work is *today's* duty; though its material is borrowed from the future, the duty, like all duties, is in the present. This is not straw splitting. He does not want men to give the Future their hearts, to place their treasures in it. We do. His ideal is a man who, having worked all day for the good of posterity (if that is his vocation) washes his mind of the whole subject, commits the issue to Heaven, and returns at once to the patience or gratitude demanded by the moment that is passing over him. But we want a man hag-ridden by the Future—haunted by visions of an imminent heaven or hell upon earth—ready to break the Enemy's commands in the present if by doing so we make him think he can attain the

C. S. LEWIS

one or avert the other—dependent for his faith on the success or failure of schemes whose end he will not live to see. We want a whole race perpetually in pursuit of the rainbow's end, never honest, nor kind, nor happy *now,* but always using as mere fuel wherewith to heap the altar of the Future every real gift which is offered them in the Present.

The Screwtape Letters
Number 15

"DO I BELIEVE?"

THE MOMENT one asks oneself "Do I believe?" all belief seems to go. I think this is because one is trying to turn round and look *at* something which is there to be used and work *from*—trying to take out one's eyes instead of keeping them in the right place and seeing *with* them. I find that it happens about other matters as well as faith. In my experience only very robust pleasures will stand the question, "Am I really enjoying this?" Or attention—the moment I begin thinking about my attention (to a book or lecture) I have *ipso facto* ceased attending. St. Paul speaks of "Faith actualized in Love." And "the heart is deceitful": you know better than I how very unreliable introspection is. I should be much more alarmed about your progress if you wrote claiming to be overflowing with Faith, Hope and Charity.

Letters of C. S. Lewis
27th September 1949

C. S. LEWIS

THE CHRISTIAN
VIEW OF SUFFERING

CHRIST said it was difficult for "the rich" to enter the Kingdom of Heaven, referring, no doubt, to "riches" in the ordinary sense. But I think it really covers riches in every sense—good fortune, health, popularity and all the things one wants to have. All these things tend— just as money tends—to make you feel independent of God, because if you have them you are happy already and contented in this life. You don't want to turn away to any- thing more, and so you try to rest in a shadowy happiness as if it could last for ever.

But God wants to give you a real and eternal happi- ness. Consequently He may have to take all these "riches" away from you: if He doesn't, you will go on relying on them. It sounds cruel, doesn't it? But I am beginning to find out that what people call the cruel doctrines are really the kindest ones in the long run. I used to think it was a "cruel" doctrine to say that troubles and sorrows were "punishments." But I find in practice that when you are in trouble, the moment you regard it as a "punishment," it be- comes easier to bear. If you think of this world as a place intended simply for our happiness, you find it quite intol- erable: think of it as a place of training and correction and it's not so bad.

Imagine a set of people all living in the same build- ing. Half of them think it is a hotel, the other half think it is a prison. Those who think it a hotel might regard it as quite intolerable, and those who thought it was a prison might decide that it was really surprisingly comfortable. So that what seems the ugly doctrine is one that comforts

and strengthens you in the end. The people who try to
hold an optimistic view of this world would become pes-
simists: the people who hold a pretty stern view of it become optimistic.

"Answers to Questions on Christianity"
in *Timeless at Heart*

C. S. LEWIS

ANXIETY

Some people feel guilty about their anxieties and regard them as a defect of faith. I don't agree at all. They are afflictions, not sins. Like all afflictions, they are, if we can so take them, our share in the Passion of Christ. For the beginning of the Passion—the first move, so to speak—is in Gethsemane. In Gethsemane a very strange and significant thing seems to have happened.

It is clear from many of His sayings that Our Lord had long foreseen His death. He knew what conduct such as His, in a world such as we have made of this, must inevitably lead to. But it is clear that this knowledge must somehow have been withdrawn from Him before He prayed in Gethsemane. He could not, with whatever reservation about the Father's will, have prayed that the cup might pass and simultaneously known that it would not. That is both a logical and a psychological impossibility. You see what this involves? Lest any trial incident to humanity should be lacking, the torments of hope—of suspense, anxiety—were at the last moment loosed upon Him—the supposed possibility that, after all, He might, He just conceivably might, be spared the supreme horror. There was a precedent. Isaac had been spared: he too at the last moment, he also against all apparent probability. It was not quite impossible . . . and doubtless He had seen other men crucified . . . a sight very unlike most of our religious pictures and images.

But for this last (and erroneous) hope against hope, and the consequent tumult of the soul, the sweat of blood, perhaps He would not have been very Man. To live in a fully predictable world is not to be a man.

Readings for Meditation and Reflection

At the end, I know, we are told that an angel appeared "comforting" Him. But neither *comforting* in sixteenth-century English nor ... in Greek means "consoling." "Strengthening" is more the word. May not the strengthening have consisted in the renewed certainty— cold comfort this—that the thing must be endured and therefore could be?

We all try to accept with some sort of submission our afflictions when they actually arrive. But the prayer in Gethsemane shows that the preceding anxiety is equally God's will and equally part of our human destiny. The perfect Man experienced it. And the servant is not greater than the master. We are Christians, not Stoics.

Letters to Malcolm
Chapter 8

GUILT

MANY modern psychologists tell us always to distrust this vague feeling of guilt, as something purely pathological. And if they had stopped at that, I might believe them. But when they go on, as some do, to apply the same treatment to all guilt-feelings whatever, to suggest that one's feeling about a particular unkind act or a particular insincerity is also and equally untrustworthy—I can't help thinking they are talking nonsense. One sees this the moment one looks at other people. I have talked to some who felt guilt when they jolly well ought to have felt it; they have behaved like brutes and know it. I've also met others who felt guilty and weren't guilty by any standard I can apply. And thirdly, I've met people who were guilty and didn't seem to feel guilt. And isn't this what we should expect? People can be *malades imaginaires* who are well and think they are ill; and others, especially consumptives, are ill and think they are well; and thirdly—far the largest class—people are ill and know they are ill. It would be very odd if there were any region in which all mistakes were in one direction.

Some Christians would tell us to go on rummaging and scratching till we find something specific. We may be sure, they say, that there are real sins enough to justify the guilt-feeling or to overthrow the feeling that all is well. I think they are right in saying that if we hunt long enough we shall find, or think we have found, something. But that is just what wakens suspicion. A theory which could never by any experience be falsified can for that reason hardly be verified. And just as, when we are yielding to temptation, we make ourselves believe that what we have always thought a sin will on this occasion, for some strange reason, not be a sin, shan't we persuade ourselves that something we have always (rightly) thought to be innocent was really wrong? We may create scruples. And scruples are always a bad thing—if only because they usually distract us from real duties.

I don't at all know whether I'm right or not, but I have, on the whole, come to the conclusion that one can't directly *do* anything about either feeling. One is not to believe either—indeed, how can one believe a fog? I come back to St. John: "if our heart condemn us, God is greater than our heart." And equally, if our heart flatter us, God is greater than our heart. I sometimes pray not for self-knowledge in general but for just so much self-knowledge at the moment as I can bear and use at the moment; the little daily dose.

Letters to Malcolm
Chapter 6

C. S. LEWIS

SCREWTAPE EXPLAINS TO WORMWOOD WHY GOD WILL NOT OVER-RIDE HUMAN FREE-WILL

You must have often wondered why the Enemy does not make more use of His power to be sensibly present to human souls in any degree He chooses and at any moment. But you now see that the Irresistible and the Indisputable are the two weapons which the very nature of His scheme forbids Him to use. Merely to over-ride a human will (as His felt presence in any but the faintest and most mitigated degree would certainly do) would be for Him useless. He cannot ravish. He can only woo. For His ignoble idea is to eat the cake and have it; the creatures are to be one with Him, but yet themselves; merely to cancel them, or assimilate them, will not serve. He is prepared to do a little over-riding at the beginning. He will set them off with communications of His presence which, though faint, seem great to them, with emotional sweetness, and easy conquest over temptation. But He never allows this state of affairs to last long.

Sooner or later He withdraws, if not in fact, at least from their conscious experience, all those supports and incentives. He leaves the creature to stand up on its own legs—to carry out from the will alone duties which have lost all relish. It is during such trough periods, much more than during the peak periods, that it is growing into the sort of creature He wants it to be. Hence the prayers offered in the state of dryness are those which please Him best. We can drag our patients along by continual tempting, because we design them only for the table, and the more their will is interfered with the better. He cannot "tempt" to virtue as we do to vice. He wants them to learn to walk and must therefore take away His hand; and if only the will to walk is really there He is pleased even with their stumbles.

Do not be deceived, Wormwood. Our cause is never more in danger than when a human, no longer desiring, but still intending, to do our Enemy's will, looks round upon a universe from which every trace of Him seems to have vanished, and asks why he has been forsaken, and still obeys.

The Screwtape Letters
Number 8

C. S. LEWIS

GIFT-LOVE AND NEED-LOVE

"GOD IS LOVE," says St. John. When I first tried to write [*The Four Loves*] I thought that his maxim would provide me with a very plain highroad through the whole subject. I thought I should be able to say that human loves deserved to be called loves at all just in so far as they resembled that Love which is God. The first distinction I made was therefore between what I called Gift-love and Need-love. The typical example of Gift-love would be that love which moves a man to work and plan and save for the future well-being of his family which he will die without sharing or seeing; of the second, that which sends a lonely or frightened child to its mother's arms.

There was no doubt which was more like Love Himself. Divine Love is Gift-love. The Father gives all He is and has to the Son. The Son gives Himself back to the Father, and gives Himself to the world, and for the world to the Father, and thus gives the world (in Himself) back to the Father too.

And what, on the other hand, can be less like anything we believe of God's life than Need-love? He lacks nothing, but our Need-love, as Plato saw, is "the son of Poverty." It is the accurate reflection in consciousness of our actual nature. We are born helpless. As soon as we are fully conscious we discover loneliness. We need others physically, emotionally, intellectually; we need them if we are to know anything, even ourselves. . . .

Every Christian would agree that a man's spiritual health is exactly proportional to his love for God. But man's love for God, from the very nature of the case, must always be very largely, and must often be entirely, a Need-love. This is obvious when we implore forgiveness for our sins or support in our tribulations. But in the long run it is perhaps even more apparent in our growing—for it ought to be growing—awareness that our whole being by its very nature is one vast need; incomplete, preparatory, empty yet cluttered, crying out for Him who can untie things that are now knotted together and tie up things that are still dangling loose. . . .

It would be a bold and silly creature that came before its Creator with the boast "I'm no beggar. I love you disinterestedly." Those who come nearest to a Gift-love for God will next moment, even at the very same moment, be beating their breasts with the publican and laying their indigence before the only real Giver. And God will have it so. He addresses our Need-love: "Come unto me all ye that travail and are heavy-laden," or, in the Old Testament, "Open your mouth wide and I will fill it" . . .

The Four Loves
Chapter 1

C. S. LEWIS

LOVE 1: AFFECTION

A FFECTION . . . is the humblest love. It gives itself no airs. People can be proud of being "in love," or of friendship. Affection is modest—even furtive and shame-faced. Once when I had remarked on the affection quite often found between cat and dog, my friend replied, "Yes. But I bet no dog would ever confess it to the other dogs." That is at least a good caricature of much human Affection. "Let homely faces stay at home," says Comus. Now Affection has a very homely face. So have many of those for whom we feel it. It is no proof of our refinement or perceptiveness that we love them; nor that they love us. . . .

It usually needs absence or bereavement to set us praising those to whom only Affection binds us. We take them for granted: and this taking for granted, which is an outrage in erotic love, is here right and proper up to a point. It fits the comfortable, quiet nature of the feeling. Affection would not be affection if it was loudly and frequently expressed; to produce it in public is like getting your household furniture out for a move. It did very well in its place, but it looks shabby or tawdry or grotesque in the sunshine. Affection almost slinks or seeps through our lives. It lives with humble, un-dress, private things; soft slippers, old clothes, old jokes, the thump of a sleepy dog's tail on the kitchen floor, the sound of a sewing machine, a gollywog left on the lawn.

But I must correct myself. I am talking of Affection as it is when it exists apart from the other loves. It often does so exist; often not. As gin is not only a drink in itself but also a base for many mixed drinks, so Affection, besides being a love itself, can enter into the other loves and color them all through and become the medium in which from day to day they operate. They would not perhaps wear very well without it. To make a friend is not the same as to become affectionate. But when your friend has become an old friend, all those things about him which had originally nothing to do with the friendship become familiar and dear with familiarity. As for erotic love, I can imagine nothing more disagreeable than to experience it for more than a very short time without this homespun clothing of affection.

The Four Loves
Chapter 3

LOVE 2: FRIENDSHIP

T HOSE who cannot conceive Friendship as a substantive love but only as a disguise or elaboration of Eros betray the fact that they have never had a Friend. The rest of us know that though we can have erotic love and friendship for the same person yet in some ways nothing is less like a Friendship than a love affair. Lovers are always talking to one another about their love; Friends hardly ever about their Friendship. Lovers are normally face to face, absorbed in each other; Friends, side by side, absorbed in some common interest. Above all, Eros (while it lasts) is necessarily between two only. But two, far from being the necessary number for Friendship, is not even the best. And the reason for this is important.

Lamb says somewhere that if, of three friends (A, B and C), A should die, then B loses not only A but "A's part in C," while C loses not only A but "A's part in B." In each of my friends there is something that only some other friend can fully bring out. By myself I am not large enough to call the whole man into activity; I want other lights than my own to show all his facets. Now that Charles is dead, I shall never again see Ronald's reaction to a specifically Caroline joke. Far from having more of Ronald, having him "to myself" now that Charles is away, I have less of Ronald. Hence true Friendship is the least jealous of loves. Two friends delight to be joined by a third, and three by a fourth, if only the newcomer is qualified to become a real friend. They can then say, as the blessed souls says in Dante, "Here comes one who will augment our loves." For in this love "to divide is not to take away" . . .

Friendship arises out of mere Companionship when two or more of the companions discover that they have in

Readings for Meditation and Reflection

common some insight or interest or even taste which the others do not share and which, till that moment, each believed to be his own unique treasure (or burden). The typical expression of opening Friendship would be something like, "What? You too? I thought I was the only one." We can imagine that among those early hunters and warriors single individuals—one in a century? One in a thousand years?—saw what others did not; saw that the deer was beautiful as well as edible, that hunting was fun as well as necessary, dreamed that his gods might be not only powerful but holy. But as long as each of these percipient persons dies without finding a kindred soul, nothing (I suspect) will come of it; art or sport or spiritual religion will not be born. It is when two such persons discover one another, when, whether with immense difficulties and semiarticulate fumblings or with what would seem to us amazing and elliptical speed, they share their vision—it is then that Friendship is born. And instantly they stand together in an immense solitude. . . .

For us of course the shared activity and therefore the companionship on which Friendship supervenes will not often be a bodily one like hunting or fighting. It may be a common religion, common studies, a common profession, even a common recreation. All who share it will be our companions; but one or two or three who share something more will be our Friends. In this kind of love, as Emerson said, *Do you love me?* means *Do you see the same truth?*—Or at least, "Do you *care* about the same truth?" The man who agrees with us that some question, little regarded by others, is of great importance, can be our Friend. He need not agree with us about the answer.

The Four Loves
Chapter 4

C. S. LEWIS

LOVE 3: EROS

By EROS I mean of course that state which we call "being in love"; if you prefer, that kind of love which lovers are "in." Some readers may have been surprised when ... I described Affection as the love in which our experience seems to come closest to that of the animals. Surely, it might be asked, our sexual functions bring us equally close? That is quite true as regards human sexuality in general. But I am not going to be concerned with human sexuality simply as such. Sexuality makes part of our subject only when it becomes an ingredient in the complex state of "being in love." That sexual experience can occur without Eros, without being "in love," and that Eros includes other things besides sexual activity, I take for granted.... The carnal or animally sexual element with Eros, I intend (following an old usage) to call Venus. And I mean by Venus what is sexual not in some cryptic or rarefied sense—such as a depth-psychologist might explore—but in a perfectly obvious sense; what is known to be sexual by those who experience it; what could be proved to be sexual by the simplest observations.

Sexuality may operate without Eros or as part of Eros. Let me hasten to add that I make the distinction simply in order to limit our inquiry and without any moral implications. I am not at all subscribing to the popular idea that it is the absence or presence of Eros which makes the sexual act "impure" or "pure," degraded or fine, unlawful or lawful. If all who lay together without being in the state of Eros were abominable, we all come of tainted stock. The times and places in which marriage depends on Eros are in a small minority. Most of our ancestors were married off in early youth to partners chosen by their parents on grounds that had nothing to do with Eros. They went to the act with no other "fuel," so to speak, than plain animal desire. And they did right; honest Christian husbands and wives, obeying their fathers and mothers, discharging to one another their "marriage debt," and bringing up families in the fear of the Lord. Conversely, this act, done under the influence of a soaring and iridescent Eros which reduces the role of the senses to a minor consideration, may yet be plain adultery, may involve breaking a wife's heart, deceiving a husband, betraying a friend, polluting hospitality and deserting your children. It has not pleased God that the distinction between a sin and a duty should turn on fine feelings.

The Four Loves
Chapter 5

THE DISTRACTIONS
OF DOMESTICITY

IT HAS been widely held in the past, and is perhaps held by many unsophisticated people today, that the spiritual danger of Eros arises almost entirely from the carnal element within it; that Eros is "noblest" or "purest" when Venus is reduced to the minimum. The older moral theologians certainly seem to have thought that the danger we chiefly had to guard against in marriage was that of a soul-destroying surrender to the senses. It will be noticed, however, that this is not the scriptural approach. St. Paul, dissuading his converts from marriage, says nothing about that side of the matter except to discourage prolonged abstinence from Venus (1 Corinthians 7:5). What he fears is preoccupation, the need of constantly "pleasing"—that is, considering—one's partner, the multiple distractions of domesticity. It is marriage itself, not the marriage bed, that will be likely to hinder us from waiting uninterruptedly on God. And surely St. Paul is right? If I may trust my own experience, it is (within marriage as without) the practical and prudential cares of this world, and even the smallest and most prosaic of those cares, that are the great distraction. The gnat-like cloud of petty anxieties and decisions about the conduct of the next hour have interfered with my prayers more often than any passion or appetite whatever. The great, permanent temptation of marriage is not to sensuality but (quite bluntly) to avarice.

The Four Loves
Chapter 5

Readings for Meditation and Reflection

BROTHER ASS

I CAN HARDLY help regarding it as one of God's jokes that a passion so soaring, so apparently transcendent, as Eros, should thus be linked in incongruous symbiosis with a bodily appetite which, like any other appetite, tactlessly reveals its connections with such mundane factors as weather, health, diet, circulation and digestion. In Eros at times we seem to be flying; Venus gives us the sudden twitch that reminds us we are really captive balloons. It is a continual demonstration of the truth that we are composite creatures, rational animals, akin on one side to the angels, on the other to tom-cats. It is a bad thing not to be able to take a joke. Worse, not to take a divine joke; made, I grant you, at our expense, but also (who doubts it?) for our endless benefit.

Man has held three views of his body. First there is that of those ascetic Pagans who called it the prison or the "tomb" of the soul, and of Christians like Fisher to whom it was a "sack of dung," food for worms, filthy, shameful, a source of nothing but temptation to bad men and humiliation to good ones. Then there are the Neo-Pagans (they seldom know Greek), the nudists and the sufferers from Dark Gods, to whom the body is glorious. But thirdly we have the view which St. Francis expressed by calling his body "Brother Ass." All three may be—I am not sure—defensible; but give me St. Francis for my money.

Ass is exquisitely right because no one in his senses can either revere or hate a donkey. It is a useful, sturdy, lazy, obstinate, patient, lovable and infuriating beast;

C. S. LEWIS

deserving now the stick and now a carrot; both pathetically and absurdly beautiful. So the body.

The Four Loves
Chapter 5

WHEN EROS
BECOMES A DEMON

Eros, honored without reservation and obeyed unconditionally, becomes a demon. And this is just how he claims to be honored and obeyed. Divinely indifferent to our selfishness, he is also demoniacally rebellious to every claim of God or Man that would oppose him. Hence as the poet says:

> People in love cannot be moved by kindness
> And opposition makes them feel like martyrs. . . .

When lovers say of some act that we might blame, "Love made us do it," notice the tone. A man saying, "I did it because I was frightened" or "I did it because I was angry," speaks quite differently. He is putting forward an excuse for what he feels to require excusing. But the lovers are seldom doing quite that. Notice how tremulously, almost how devoutly, they say the word *love,* not so much pleading an "extenuating circumstance" as appealing to an authority. The confession can be almost a boast. There can be a shade of defiance in it. They "feel like martyrs." In extreme cases what their words really express is a demure yet unshakable allegiance to the god of love.

"These reasons in love's law have passed for good," says Milton's Dalila. That is the point; *in love's law.* "In love," we have our own "law," a religion of our own, our own god. Where a true Eros is present resistance to his commands feels like apostasy, and what are really (by the Christian standard) temptations speak with the voice of duties—quasi-religious duties, acts of pious zeal to Love. He builds his own religion round the lovers. . . .

C. S. LEWIS

The "spirit" of Eros . . . seems to sanction all sorts of actions they would not otherwise have dared. I do not mean solely, or chiefly, acts that violate chastity. They are just as likely to be acts of injustice or uncharity against the outer world. They will seem like proofs of piety and zeal towards Eros. The pair can say to one another in an almost sacrificial spirit, "It is for love's sake that I have neglected my parents—left my children—cheated my partner—failed my friend at his greatest need." These reasons in love's law have passed for good. The votaries may even come to feel a particular merit in such sacrifices; what costlier offering can be laid on love's altar than one's conscience?

The Four Loves
Chapter 5

LOVE 4: CHARITY

In GOD there is no hunger that needs to be filled, only plenteousness that desires to give. The doctrine that God was under no necessity to create is not a piece of dry scholastic speculation. It is essential. Without it we can hardly avoid the conception of what I can only call a "managerial" God; a Being whose function or nature is to "run" the universe, who stands to it as a headmaster to a school or a hotelier to a hotel. But to be sovereign of the universe is no great matter to God. In Himself, at home in "the land of the Trinity," He is Sovereign of a far greater realm. We must keep always before our eyes that vision of Lady Julian's in which God carried in His hand a little object like a nut, and that nut was "all that is made." God, who needs nothing, loves into existence wholly superfluous creatures in order that He may love and perfect them. He creates the universe, already foreseeing—or should we say "seeing"?, there are no tenses in God—the buzzing cloud of flies about the cross, the flayed back pressed against the uneven stake, the nails driven through the mesial nerves, the repeated incipient suffocation as the body droops, the repeated torture of back and arms as it is time after time, for breath's sake, hitched up. If I may dare the biological image, God is a "host" who deliberately creates His own parasites; causes us to be that we may exploit and "take advantage of" Him. Herein is love. This is the diagram of Love Himself, the inventor of all loves. . . .

In addition to these natural loves God . . . communicates to men a share of His own Gift-love. This is different from the Gift-loves He has built into their nature. These never quite seek simply the good of the loved object for the object's own sake. They are biased in favor of those goods

C. S. LEWIS

they can themselves bestow, or those which they would like best themselves, or those which fit in with a pre-conceived picture of the life they want the object to lead. But Divine Gift-love—Love Himself working in a man—is wholly disinterested and desires what is simply best for the beloved. Again, natural Gift-love is always directed to objects which the lover finds in some way intrinsically lovable—objects to which Affection or Eros or a shared point of view attracts him, or failing that, to the grateful and the deserving, or perhaps to those whose helplessness is of a winning and appealing kind. But Divine Gift-love in the man enables him to love what is not naturally lovable: lepers, criminals, enemies, morons, the sulky, the superior and the sneering.

Finally, by a high paradox, God enables men to have a Gift-love towards Himself. There is of course a sense in which no one can give to God anything which is not already His; and if it is already His, what have you given? But since it is only too obvious that we can withhold ourselves, our wills and hearts, from God, we can, in that sense, also give them. What is His by right and would not exist for a moment if it ceased to be His (as the song is the singer's), He has nevertheless made ours in such a way that we can freely offer it back to Him.

The Four Loves
Chapter 6

SUPERNATURAL NEED-LOVE OF GOD AND OF ONE ANOTHER

THAT such a Gift-love comes by Grace and should be called Charity, everyone will agree ... God, as it seems to me, bestows two other gifts: a supernatural Need-love of Himself and a supernatural Need-love of one another. ... Let us consider first this supernatural Need-love of Himself, bestowed by Grace. Of course the Grace does not create the need. That is there already; "given" (as the mathematicians say) in the mere fact of our being creatures, and incalculably increased by our being fallen creatures. What the Grace gives is the full recognition, the sensible awareness, the complete acceptance—even, with certain reservations, the glad acceptance—of this Need. For, without Grace, our wishes and our necessities are in conflict. ...

No sooner do we believe that God loves us than there is an impulse to believe that he does so, not because He is Love, but because we are intrinsically lovable. ... Thus, depth beneath depth and subtlety within subtlety, there remains some lingering idea of our own, our very own, attractiveness. It is easy to acknowledge, but almost impossible to realize for long, that we are mirrors whose brightness, if we are bright, is wholly derived from the sun that shines upon us. Surely we must have a little—however little—native luminosity? Surely we can't be *quite* creatures? For this tangled absurdity of a Need, even a Need-love, which never fully acknowledges its own neediness, Grace substitutes a full, childlike and delighted acceptance of our Need, a joy in total dependence. We become "jolly beggars" ...

C. S. LEWIS

But God also transforms our Need-love for one another. . . . How difficult it is to receive, and to go on receiving, from others a love that does not depend on our own attraction, can be seen from an extreme case. Suppose yourself a man struck down shortly after marriage by an incurable disease which may not kill you for many years; useless, impotent, hideous, disgusting; dependent on your wife's earnings; impoverishing where you hoped to enrich; impaired even in intellect and shaken by gusts of uncontrollable temper, full of unavoidable demands. And suppose your wife's care and pity to be inexhaustible. The man who can take this sweetly, who can receive all and give nothing without resentment, who can abstain even from those tiresome self-deprecations which are really only a demand for petting and reassurance, is doing something which Need-love in its merely natural condition could not attain. . . . In such a case to receive is harder and perhaps more blessed than to give. But what the extreme example illustrates is universal. We are all receiving Charity. There is something in each of us that cannot be naturally loved. It is not one's fault if they do not so love it. Only the lovable can be naturally loved. You might as well ask people to like the taste of rotten bread or the sound of a mechanical drill. We can be forgiven, and pitied, and loved in spite of it, with Charity; no other way. All who have good parents, wives, husbands, or children, may be sure that at some time—and perhaps at all times in respect of some one particular trait or habit—they are receiving charity, are loved not because they are lovable but because Love Himself is in those who love them.

The Four Loves
Chapter 6

Readings for Meditation and Reflection

"HATING" THE
PEOPLE WE LOVE

As so often, Our Lord's own words are both far fiercer and far more tolerable than those of the theologians. He says nothing about guarding against earthly loves for fear we might be hurt; He says something that cracks like a whip about trampling them all under foot the moment they hold us back from following Him. "If any man come to me and hate not his father and mother and wife . . . and his own life also, he cannot be my disciple" (Luke 14:26).

But how are we to understand the word *hate*? That Love Himself should be commanding what we ordinarily mean by hatred—commanding us to cherish resentment, to gloat over another's misery, to delight in injuring him—is almost a contradiction in terms. I think Our Lord, in the sense here intended, "hated" St. Peter when He said, "Get thee behind me." To hate is to reject, to set one's face against, to make no concession to, the Beloved when the Beloved utters, however sweetly and however pitiably, the suggestions of the Devil. A man, said Jesus, who tries to serve two masters, will "hate" the one and "love" the other. It is not, surely, mere feelings of aversion and liking that are here in question. . . .

In the last resort, we must turn down or disqualify our nearest and dearest when they come between us and our obedience to God. Heaven knows, it will seem to them sufficiently like hatred. We must not act on the pity we feel; we must be blind to tears and deaf to pleadings.

I will not say that this duty is hard; some find it too easy; some, hard almost beyond endurance. What is hard for all is to know when the occasion for such "hating" has

C. S. LEWIS

arisen. Our temperaments deceive us. The meek and tender—uxorious husbands, submissive wives, doting parents, dutiful children—will not easily believe that it has ever arrived. Self-assertive people, with a dash of the bully in them, will believe it too soon. That is why it is of such extreme importance so to order our loves that it is unlikely to arrive at all.

The Four Loves
Chapter 6

TO LOVE IS TO BE VULNERABLE

To love at all is to be vulnerable. Love anything, and your heart will certainly be wrung and possibly be broken. If you want to make sure of keeping it intact, you must give your heart to no one, not even to an animal. Wrap it carefully round with hobbies and little luxuries, avoid all entanglements, lock it up safe in the casket or coffin of your selfishness. But in that casket—safe, dark, motionless, airless—it will change. It will not be broken; it will become unbreakable, impenetrable, irredeemable. The alternative to tragedy, or at least to the risk of tragedy, is damnation. The only place outside Heaven where you can be perfectly safe from all the dangers and perturbations of love is Hell.

I believe that the most lawless and inordinate loves are less contrary to God's will than a self-invited and self-protective lovelessness. It is like hiding the talent in a napkin and for much the same reason. "I knew thee that thou wert a hard man." Christ did not teach and suffer that we might become, even in the natural loves, more careful of our own happiness. If a man is not uncalculating towards the earthly beloveds whom he has seen, he is none the more likely to be so towards God whom he has not. We shall draw nearer to God, not by trying to avoid the sufferings inherent in all loves, but by accepting them and offering them to Him; throwing away all defensive armour. If our hearts need to be broken, and if He chooses this as the way in which they should break, so be it.

The Four Loves
Chapter 6

C. S. LEWIS

CONSCIOUSNESS OF SIN

CHRIST takes it for granted that men are bad. Until we really feel this assumption of His to be true, though we are part of the world He came to save, we are not part of the audience to whom His words are addressed. We lack the first condition for understanding what He is talking about. And when men attempt to be Christians without this preliminary consciousness of sin, the result is almost bound to be a certain resentment against God as to one who is always making impossible demands and always inexplicably angry. Most of us have at times felt a secret sympathy with the dying farmer who replied to the Vicar's dissertation on repentance by asking, "What harm have I ever done *Him?*" There is the real rub. The worst we have done to God is to leave Him alone—why can't He return the compliment? Why not live and let live? What call had He, of all beings, to be "angry"? It's easy for Him to be good!

Now at the moment when a man feels real guilt— moments too rare in our lives—all these blasphemies vanish away. Much, we may feel, can be excused to human infirmities: but not *this*—this incredibly mean and ugly action which none of our friends would have done, which even such a thorough-going little rotter as X would have been ashamed of, which we would not for the world allow to be published. At such a moment we really do know that our character, as revealed in this action, is, and ought to be, hateful to all good men, and, if there are powers above man, to them. A God who did not regard this with unappeasable distaste would not be a good being. We cannot even wish for such a God—it is like wishing that every nose in the universe were abolished, that the smell of hay or roses or the sea should never again delight any creature, because our own breath happens to stink.

When we merely *say* that we are bad, the "wrath" of God seems a barbarous doctrine; as soon as we *perceive* our badness, it appears inevitable, a mere corollary from God's goodness. To keep ever before us the insight derived from such a moment as I have been describing, to learn to detect the same real inexcusable corruption under more and more of its complex disguises, is therefore indispensable to a real understanding of the Christian faith.

The Problem of Pain
Chapter 4

THE CENTRAL SELF

CHRISTIAN writers . . . seem to be so very strict at one moment and so very free and easy at another. They talk about mere sins of thought as if they were immensely important, and then they talk about the most frightful murders and treacheries as if you had only got to repent and all would be forgiven. But I have come to see that they are right. What they are always thinking of is the mark which the action leaves on that tiny central self which no one sees in this life but which each of us will have to endure—or enjoy—forever. One man may be so placed that however angry he gets he will only be laughed at. But the little mark on the soul may be much the same in both. Each has done something to himself which, unless he repents, will make it harder for him to keep out of the rage next time he is tempted, and will make the rage worse when he does fall into it. Each of them, if he seriously turns to God, can have that twist in the central man straightened out again: each is, in the long run, doomed if he will not. The bigness or smallness of the thing, seen from the outside, is not what really matters. . . .

The right direction leads not only to peace but to knowledge. When a man is getting better he understands more and more clearly the evil that is still left in him. When a man is getting worse, he understands his own badness less and less. A moderately bad man knows he is not very good: a thoroughly bad man thinks he is all right. This is common sense, really. You understand sleep when you are awake, not while you are sleeping. You can see mistakes in arithmetic when your mind is working properly: while you are making them you cannot see them. You

can understand the nature of drunkenness when you are
sober, not when you are drunk. Good people know about
both good and evil: bad people do not know about either.

Mere Christianity
Book III Chapter 4

C. S. LEWIS

A FIFTH-COLUMNIST
IN THE SOUL

J UST as the Christian has his moments when the clamor of this visible and audible world is so persistent and the whisper of the spiritual world so faint that faith and reason can hardly stick to their guns, so, as I well remember, the atheist too has his moments of shuddering misgiving, of an all but irresistible suspicion that old tales may after all be true, that something or someone from outside may at any moment break into his neat, explicable, mechanical universe. Believe in God and you will have to face hours when it seems *obvious* that this material world is the only reality: disbelieve in Him and you must face hours when this material world seems to shout at you that it is *not* all. No conviction, religious or irreligious, will, of itself, end once and for all this fifth-columnist in the soul. Only the practice of Faith resulting in the habit of Faith will gradually do that. . . .

When we exhort people to Faith as a virtue, to the settled intention of continuing to believe certain things, we are not exhorting them to fight against reason. The intention of continuing to believe is required because, though Reason is divine, human reasoners are not. When once passion takes part in the game, the human reason, unassisted by Grace, has about as much chance of retaining its hold on truths already gained as a snow-flake has of retaining its consistency in the mouth of a blast furnace. The sort of arguments against Christianity which our reason can be persuaded to accept at the moment of yielding to temptation are often preposterous. Reason may win truths; without Faith she will retain them just so long as Satan pleases.

Readings for Meditation and Reflection

There is nothing we cannot be made to believe or disbelieve. If we wish to be rational, not now and then, but constantly, we must pray for the gift of Faith, for the power to go on believing not in the teeth of reason but in the teeth of lust and terror and jealously and boredom and indifference that which reason, authority, or experience, or all three, have once delivered to us for truth. And the answer to that prayer will, perhaps, surprise us when it comes. For I am not sure, after all, whether one of the causes of our weak faith is not a secret wish that our faith should *not* be very strong. Is there some reservation in our minds? Some fear of what it might be like if our religion became *quite* real? I hope not. God help us all, and forgive us.

"Religion: Reality or Substitute?"
in *Christian Reflections*

C. S. LEWIS

A CAUTION

I KNOW all about the despair of overcoming chronic temptation. It is not serious, provided self-offended petulance, annoyance at breaking records, impatience, etc., don't get the upper hand. No *amount* of falls will really undo us if we keep on picking ourselves up each time. We shall of course be very muddy and tattered children by the time we reach home. But the bathrooms are all ready, the towels put out, and the clean clothes in the airing cupboard. The only fatal thing is to lose one's temper and give it up. It is when we notice the dirt that God is most present in us: it is the very sign of His presence.

Letters of C. S. Lewis
20th January 1942

NICE PEOPLE OR NEW MEN

I f you have sound nerves and intelligence and health and popularity and a good upbringing, you are likely to be quite satisfied with your character as it is. "Why drag God into it?" you may ask. A certain level of good conduct comes fairly easily to you. You are not one of those wretched creatures who are always being tripped up by sex, or dipsomania, or nervousness, or bad temper. Everyone says you are a nice chap and (between ourselves) you agree with them. You are quite likely to believe that all this niceness is your own doing: and you may easily not feel the need for any better kind of goodness. Often people who have all these natural kinds of goodness cannot be brought to recognize their need for Christ at all until, one day, the natural goodness lets them down and their self-satisfaction is shattered. In other words, it is hard for those who are "rich" in this sense to enter the Kingdom. . . .

If you are a nice person—if virtue comes easily to you—beware! Much is expected from those to whom much is given. If you mistake for your own merits what are really God's gifts to you through nature, and if you are contented with simply being nice, you are still a rebel: and all those gifts will only make your fall more terrible, your corruption more complicated, your bad example more disastrous. The Devil was an archangel once; his natural gifts were as far above yours as yours are above those of a chimpanzee.

But if you are a poor creature—poisoned by a wretched upbringing in some house full of vulgar jealousies and senseless quarrels—saddled, by no choice of your own, with some loathsome sexual perversion—nagged day in and day out by an inferiority complex that makes

C. S. LEWIS

you snap at your best friends—do not despair. He knows all about it. You are one of the poor whom He blessed. He knows what a wretched machine you are trying to drive. Keep on. Do what you can. One day (perhaps in another world, but perhaps sooner than that) He will fling it on the scrap-heap and give you a new one. And then you may astonish us all—not least yourself: for you have learned your driving in a hard school. (Some of the last will be first and some of the first will be last.)

"Niceness"—wholesome, integrated personality—is an excellent thing. We must try by every medical, educational, economic and political means in our power, to produce a world where as many people as possible grow up "nice"; just as we must try to produce a world where all have plenty to eat. But we must not suppose that even if we succeeded in making everyone nice we should have saved their souls. A world of nice people, content in their own niceness, looking no further, turned away from God, would be just as desperately in need of salvation as a miserable world—and might even be more difficult to save.

For mere improvement is not redemption, though redemption always improves people even here and now and will, in the end, improve them to a degree we cannot yet imagine. God became man to turn creatures into sons: not simply to produce better men of the old kind but to produce a new kind of man. It is not like teaching a horse to jump better and better but like turning a horse into a winged creature.

Mere Christianity
Book iv Chapter 10

THE PERFECT CRITIQUE

Our ancestors had a habit of using the word "judgment" . . . as if it meant simply "punishment": hence the popular expression, "It's a judgment on him." I believe we can sometimes render the thing more vivid to ourselves by taking judgment in a stricter sense: not as the sentence or award, but as the verdict. Some day (and "What if this present were the world's last night?") an absolutely correct verdict—if you like, a perfect critique—will be passed on what each of us is.

We have all encountered judgments or verdicts on ourselves in this life. Every now and then we discover what our fellow creatures really think of us. I don't of course mean what they tell us to our faces: that we usually have to discount. I am thinking of what we sometimes overhear by accident or of the opinions about us which our neighbors or employees or subordinates unknowingly reveal in their actions; and of the terrible, or lovely, judgments artlessly betrayed by children or even animals. Such discoveries can be the bitterest or sweetest experiences we have. But of course both the bitter and the sweet are limited by our doubt as to the wisdom of those who judge. We always hope that those who so clearly think us cowards or bullies are ignorant and malicious; we always fear that those who trust us or admire us are misled by partiality. I suppose the experience of the final judgment (which may break in upon us at any moment) will be like these little experiences, but magnified to the Nth.

For it will be infallible judgment. If it is favorable we shall have no fear, if unfavorable, no hope that it is wrong. We shall not only believe, we shall know, beyond doubt in every fiber of our appalled or delighted being, that as the

Judge has said, so we are: neither more nor less nor other. We shall perhaps even realize that in some dim fashion we could have known it all along. We shall know and all creation will know too: our ancestors, our parents, our wives or husbands, our children. The unanswerable and (by then) self-evident truth about each will be known to all.

I do not find that pictures of physical catastrophe— that sign in the clouds, those heavens rolled up like a scroll—help one so much as the naked idea of judgment. We cannot always be excited. We can, perhaps, train ourselves to ask more and more often how the thing which we are saying or doing (or failing to do) at each moment will look when the irresistible light streams in upon it; that light which is so different from the light of this world— and yet, even now, we know just enough of it to take it into account. Women sometimes have the problem of trying to judge by artificial light how a dress will look by daylight. That is very like the problem of all of us: to dress our souls not for the electric lights of the present world but for the daylight of the next. The good dress is the one that will face that light. For that light will last longer.

"The World's Last Night"
in *Fern-seed and Elephants*

THE SECOND COMING

I N *King Lear* (III: vii) there is a man who is such a minor character that Shakespeare has not given him even a name: he is merely "First Servant." All the characters around him—Regan, Cornwall and Edmund—have fine, long-term plans. They think they know how the story is going to end, and they are quite wrong. The servant has no such delusions. He has no notion how the play is going to go. But he understands the present scene. He sees an abomination (the blinding of old Gloucester) taking place. He will not stand it. His sword is out and pointed at his master's breast in a moment: then Regan stabs him dead from behind. That is his whole part: eight lines all told. But if it were real life and not a play, that is the part it would be best to have acted.

The doctrine of the Second Coming teaches us that we do not and cannot know when the world drama will end. The curtain may be rung down at any moment: say, before you have finished reading this paragraph. This seems to some people intolerably frustrating. So many things would be interrupted. Perhaps you were going to get married next month, perhaps you were going to get a raise next week: you may be on the verge of a great scientific discovery: you may be maturing great social and political reforms. Surely no good and wise God would be so very unreasonable as to cut all this short? Not *now*, of all moments!

But we think thus because we keep on assuming that we know the play. We do not know the play. We do not even know whether we are in Act I or Act V. The Author knows. The audience, if there is an audience (if angels and archangels and all the company of Heaven fill the pit and the stalls), may have an inkling. But we, never seeing the play from outside, never meeting the characters except the tiny minority who are "on" in the same scenes as ourselves, wholly ignorant of the future and very imperfectly informed about the past, cannot tell at what moment the end ought to come. That it will come when it ought, we may be sure; but we waste our time in guessing when that will be. That it has a meaning we may be sure, but we cannot see it. When it is over, we may be told. We are led to expect that the Author will have something to say to each of us on the part that each of us has played. The playing it well is what matters infinitely.

The doctrine of the Second Coming, then, is not to be rejected because it conflicts with our favorite modern mythology. It is, for that very reason, to be the more valued and made more frequently the subject of meditation. It is the medicine our condition especially needs.

"The World's Last Night"
in *Fern-seed and Elephants*

THE SECRET WE CANNOT
HIDE AND CANNOT TELL

IN SPEAKING of this desire for our own far-off country, which we find in ourselves even now, I feel a certain shyness. I am almost committing an inde-cency. I am trying to rip open the inconsolable secret in each one of you—the secret which hurts so much that you take your revenge on it by calling it names like Nostalgia and Romanticism and Adolescence; the secret also which pierces with such sweetness that when, in very intimate conversation, the mention of it becomes imminent, we grow awkward and affect to laugh at ourselves; the secret we cannot hide and cannot tell, though we desire to do both. We cannot tell it because it is a desire for something that has never actually appeared in our experience. We cannot hide it because our experience is constantly suggest-ing it, and we betray ourselves like lovers at the mention of a name. Our commonest expedient is to call it beauty and behave as if that had settled the matter.

Wordsworth's expedient was to identify it with cer-tain moments in his own past. But all this is a cheat. If Wordsworth had gone back to those moments in the past, he would not have found the thing itself, but only the re-minder of it; what he remembered would turn out to be it-self a remembering. The books or the music in which we thought the beauty was located will betray us if we trust to them; it was not *in* them, it only came *through* them, and what came through them was longing. These things . . . are only the scent of a flower we have not found, the echo of a tune we have not heard, news from a country we have never yet visited.

C. S. LEWIS

Do you think I am trying to weave a spell? Perhaps I am; but remember your fairy tales. Spells are used for breaking enchantments as well as for inducing them. And you and I have need of the strongest spell that can be found to wake us from the evil enchantment of worldliness which has been laid upon us for nearly a hundred years. Almost our whole education has been directed to silencing this shy, persistent, inner voice; almost all our modern philosophies have been devised to convince us that the good of man is to be found on this earth. . . .

Do what they will, then, we remain conscious of a desire which no natural happiness will satisfy. But is there any reason to suppose that reality offers any satisfaction to it? "Nor does the being hungry prove that we have bread." But I think it may be urged that this misses the point. A man's physical hunger does not prove that that man will get any bread; he may die of starvation on a raft in the Atlantic. But surely a man's hunger does prove that he comes of a race which repairs its body by eating and inhabits a world where eatable substances exist. In the same way, though I do not believe (I wish I did) that my desire for Paradise proves that I shall enjoy it, I think it a pretty good indication that such a thing exists and that some men will.

"The Weight of Glory"
in *Screwtape Proposes a Toast*

Readings for Meditation and Reflection

FIRST AND LAST LOVE

A RE NOT all lifelong friendships born at the moment when at last you meet another human being who has some inkling (but faint and uncertain even in the best) of that something which you were born desiring, and which, beneath the flux of other desires and in all the momentary silences between the louder passions, night and day, year by year, from childhood to old age, you are looking for, watching for, listening for?

You have never *had* it. All the things that have ever deeply possessed your soul have been but hints of it—tantalizing glimpses, promises never quite fulfilled, echoes that died away just as they caught your ear. But if it should really become manifest—if there ever came an echo that did not die away but welled into the sound itself—you would know it. Beyond all possibility of doubt you would say, "Here at last is the thing I was made for." We cannot tell each other about it. It is the secret signature of each soul, the incommunicable and unappeasable want, the thing we desired before we met our wives or made our friends or chose our work, and which we shall still desire on our deathbeds, when the mind no longer knows wife or friend or work. While we are, this is. If we lose this, we lose all.

This signature on each soul may be a product of heredity and environment, but that only means that heredity and environment are among the instruments whereby God creates a soul. I am considering not how, but why, He makes each soul unique. If he had no use for all these differences, I do not see why He should have created more souls than one. Be sure that the ins and outs of your individuality are no mystery to Him; and one day they will no

C. S. LEWIS

longer be a mystery to you. The mold in which a key is made would be a strange thing, if you had never seen a key: and the key itself a strange thing if you had never seen a lock. Your soul has a curious shape because it is a hollow made to fit a particular swelling in the infinite contours of the Divine substance, or a key to unlock one of the doors in the house with many mansions. For it is not humanity in the abstract that is to be saved, but you—you, the individual reader, John Stubbs or Janet Smith. Blessed and fortunate creatures, your eyes shall behold Him and not another's. All that you are, sins apart, is destined, if you will let God have His good way, to utter satisfaction. The Brocken specter "looked to every man like his first love" because she was a cheat. But God will look to every soul like its first love because He is its first love. Your place in Heaven will seem to be made for you and you alone, because you were made for it—made for it stitch by stitch as a glove is made for a hand.

The Problem of Pain
Chapter 10

PURGATORY

Our souls *demand* Purgatory, don't they? Would it not break the heart if God said to us, "It is true, my son, that your breath smells and your rags drip with mud and slime, but we are charitable here and no one will upbraid you with these things, nor draw away from you. Enter into the joy"? Should we not reply, "With submission, sir, and if there is no objection, I'd *rather* be cleaned first." "It may hurt, you know"—"Even so, sir."

I assume that the process of purification will normally involve suffering. Partly from tradition; partly because most real good that has been done me in this life has involved it. But I don't think suffering is the purpose of the purgation. I can well believe that people neither much worse nor much better than I will suffer less than I or more. "No nonsense about merit." The treatment given will be the one required, whether it hurts little or much.

My favorite image on this matter comes from the dentist's chair. I hope that when the tooth of life is drawn and I am "coming round," a voice will say, "Rinse your mouth out with this." *This* will be Purgatory.

Letters to Malcolm
Chapter 20

C. S. LEWIS

NEW MEN IN CHRIST

To become new men means losing what we now call "ourselves." Out of ourselves, into Christ, we must go. His will is to become ours and we are to think His thoughts, to "have the mind of Christ" as the Bible says. And if Christ is one, and if He is thus to be "in" us all, shall we not be exactly the same? It certainly sounds like it; but in fact it is not so. . . .

Suppose a person who knew nothing about salt. You give him a pinch to taste and he experiences a particular strong, sharp taste. You then tell him that in your country people use salt in all their cookery. Might he not reply, "In that case I suppose all your dishes taste exactly the same: because the taste of that stuff you have just given me is so strong that it will kill the taste of everything else." But you and I know that the real effect of salt is exactly the opposite. So far from killing the taste of the egg and the tripe and the cabbage, it actually brings it out. . . .

It is something like that with Christ and us. The more we get what we now call "ourselves" out of the way and let Him take us over, the more truly ourselves we become. There is so much of Him that millions and millions of "little Christs," all different, will still be too few to express Him fully. He made them all. He invented—as an author invents characters in a novel—all the different men that you and I were intended to be. In that sense our real selves are all waiting for us in Him. It is no good trying to "be ourselves" without Him. . . . It is when I turn to Christ, when I give myself up to His Personality, that I first begin to have a real personality of my own. . . .

But there must be a real giving up of the self. You must throw it away "blindly" so to speak. Christ will indeed give you a real personality: but you must not go to Him for the sake of that. As long as your own personality is what you are bothering about you are not going to Him at all. The very first step is to try to forget about the self altogether. The real, new self (which is Christ's and also yours, and yours just because it is His) will not come as long as you are looking for it. It will come when you are looking for Him. Does that sound strange? The same principle holds, you know, for more everyday matters. Even in social life, you will never make a good impression on other people until you stop thinking about what sort of impression you are making. Even in literature and art, no man who bothers about originality will ever be original: whereas if you simply try to tell the truth (without caring tuppence how often it has been told before) you will, nine times out of ten, become original without ever having noticed it. The principle runs through all life from top to bottom. Give up your self, and you will find your real self. Lose your life and you will save it. Submit to death, death of your ambitions and favorite wishes every day and death of your whole body in the end: submit with every fiber of your being, and you will find eternal life. Keep back nothing. Nothing in you that has not died will ever be raised from the dead. Look for yourself, and you will find in the long run only hatred, loneliness, despair, rage, ruin, and decay. But look for Christ and you will find Him, and with Him everything else thrown in.

Mere Christianity
Book IV Chapter 11

C. S. LEWIS

HEAVEN

OUR NOTION of Heaven involves perpetual negations: no food, no drink, no sex, no movement, no mirth, no events, no time, no art. Against all these, to be sure, we set one positive: the vision and enjoyment of God. And since this is an infinite good, we hold (rightly) that it outweighs them all. That is, the reality of the Beatific Vision would or will outweigh, would infinitely outweigh, the reality of the negations. But can our present notion of it outweigh our present notion of them? That is quite a different question. And for most of us at most times the answer is No. How it may be for great saints and mystics I cannot tell. But for others the conception of that Vision is a difficult, precarious, and fugitive extrapolation from a very few and ambiguous moments in our earthly experience, while our idea of the negated natural goods is vivid and persistent, loaded with the great memories of a lifetime, built into our nerves and muscles and therefore into our imaginations.

Thus the negatives have, so to speak, an unfair advantage in every competition with the positive. What is worse, their presence—and most when we most resolutely try to suppress or ignore them—vitiates even such a faint and ghostlike notion of the positive as we might have had. The exclusion of the lower good begins to seem the essential characteristic of the higher good. We feel, if we do not say, that the vision of God will come not to fulfill but to destroy our nature; this bleak fantasy often underlines our very use of such words as "holy" or "pure" or "spiritual" . . .

Let us picture a woman thrown into a dungeon. There she bears and rears a son. He grows up seeing nothing but the dungeon wall, the straw on the floor, and a little patch of the sky seen through the grating, which is too high up to show anything except sky. This unfortunate woman was an artist, and when they imprisoned her she managed to bring with her a drawing pad and a box of pencils. As she never loses the hope of deliverance she is constantly teaching her son about that outer world which he has never seen. She does it very largely by drawing him pictures. With her pencil she attempts to show him what fields, rivers, mountains, cities and waves on a beach are like. He is a dutiful boy and he does his best to believe her when she tells him that that outer world is far more interesting and glorious than anything in the dungeon. At times he succeeds. On the whole he gets on tolerably well until, one day, he says something that gives his mother pause. For a minute or two they are at cross-purposes. Finally it dawns on her that he has, all these years, lived under a misconception. "But," she gasps, "you didn't think that the real world was full of lines drawn in lead pencil?" "What?," says the boy. "No pencil marks there?" And instantly his whole notion of the outer world becomes a blank. For the lines by which alone he was imagining it, have now been denied of it. He has no idea of that which will exclude and dispense with the lines, that of which the lines were merely a transposition—the waving treetops, the light dancing on the weir, the colored three-dimensional realities which are not enclosed in lines but define their own shapes at every moment with a delicacy and multiplicity which no drawing could ever achieve. The child will get the idea that the real world is somehow less visible than his mother's picture. In reality it lacks lines because it is incomparably more visible.

So with us. "We know not what we shall be"; but we may be sure we shall be more, not less, than we were

C. S. LEWIS

on earth. Our natural experiences (sensory, emotional, imaginative) are only like the drawing, like penciled lines on flat paper. If they vanish in the risen life, they will vanish only as pencil lines vanish from the real landscape; not as a candle flame that is put out but as a candle flame which becomes invisible because someone has pulled up the blind, thrown open the shutters, and let in the blaze of the risen sun.

"Transposition"
in *Screwtape Proposes a Toast*

A FINAL WORD FROM ASLAN

Here on the mountain I have spoken to you clearly: I will not often do so down in Narnia. Here on the mountain, the air is clear and your mind is clear; as you drop down into Narnia, the air will thicken. Take great care that it does not confuse your mind. And the signs which you have learned here will not look at all as you expect them to look, when you meet them there. That is why it is so important to know them by heart and pay no attention to appearances. Remember the signs and believe the signs. Nothing else matters."

The Silver Chair
Chapter 2

C. S. LEWIS

ACKNOWLEDGMENTS

Excerpts from *Christian Reflections* by C. S. Lewis copyright © 1967 by the Executors of the estate of C. S. Lewis, reprinted by permission of Wm. B. Eerdmans Publishing Company.

Excerpts from *The Four Loves* by C. S. Lewis copyright © 1960 by Helen Joy Lewis and renewed 1988 by Arthur Owen Barfield, reprinted by permission of Harcourt Brace & Company.

Excerpts from *God in the Dock* by C. S. Lewis copyright © 1970 by C. S. Lewis PTE Ltd.

Excerpts from *The Great Divorce* by C. S. Lewis copyright © 1946 by C. S. Lewis, reprinted by permission of HarperCollins Publishers Ltd.

Excerpts from *Letters of C. S. Lewis* copyright © 1966 by W. H. Lewis and the Executors of C. S. Lewis and renewed 1994 by C. S. Lewis PTE Ltd., reprinted by permission of Harcourt Brace & Company.

Excerpts from *Letters to Malcolm: Chiefly on Prayer* by C. S. Lewis copyright © 1964, 1963 by the Estate of C. S. Lewis and renewed 1992 by C. S. Lewis PTE Ltd. and 1991 by Arthur Owen Barfield, reprinted by permission of Harcourt Brace & Company.

Excerpts from *Miracles* by C. S. Lewis copyright © 1947 by C. S. Lewis, reprinted by permission of HarperCollins Publishers Ltd.

Excerpts from *The Problem of Pain* by C. S. Lewis copyright © 1940 by C. S. Lewis, reprinted by permission of HarperCollins Publishers Ltd.

Excerpts from *Reflections on the Psalms* by C. S. Lewis copyright © 1958 by C. S. Lewis and renewed 1986